Reasons *for* Believing

Reasons *for* Believing

"...be ready always to give an answer to every man that asketh you a reason of the hope that is in you..."
I Peter 3:15 (KJV)

Robert M. Tenery

Reasons For Believing
Copyright© 2016
by Robert M. Tenery

Printed in the United States of America

ISBN: 978-1530695232

All scriptures are from The New King James Version of the Bible unless otherwise noted.

Operation Transformation

Dedication

This book is dedicated to my wife, Willo'deane Foster Tenery, whose help in preparation of the manuscript for publication was indispensable.

Table of Contents

Foreword

This book is a valuable resource that will deepen and strengthen the beliefs of Christians as well as to provide them with the resolve, knowledge and skills to make Disciples of unbelievers. Jesus said in Matthew 28:19-20, *"Go, therefore, and **make disciples** of all nations, baptizing them in the name of the Father, and of the Son, and of the Holy Spirit, teaching them to observe everything I have commanded you. And remember, I am with you always, to the end of the age."* (HCSB) One can surmise from this passage that Jesus was teaching that discipleship was the task of the local church. In fact, it is implied that growing in Christ is the key to growing a healthy church. To put it another way, growing churches are discipling churches.

The church, however, is reaping the harvest of many years of neglecting discipleship. The facts speak for themselves when 86 to 93% of Evangelical churches in America are either plateauing or declining while 3,000 to 4,000 churches close their doors every year. It is clear that we must renew our commitment to discipleship in the local church.

However, it seems as if the church has decided that discipleship is no longer worth our attention. It is clear that when the church fails to make disciples the church is filled with spiritual babies that have little understanding of what it is to live with clarity the Christian life.

The truth is that when a church actively disciples the membership people will understand that stewardship is a real act of worship, Bible study is a life giving process, being an active witness is a command of Christ, prayer is the lifeline for the believer, worship is a time for refueling, and missions becomes the heartbeat of the church.

There is no doubt that Jesus entrusted the work of discipleship to the twelve who followed Him closely. He focused on training the twelve so they would win and train others. Jesus intended for this to be an ongoing process that will engulf the church and change the world. Discipleship was foundational to the ministry of Jesus and He intended it to be foundational for the church as well.

Robert Tenery has written this decisive work on discipleship. This book revisits the basic discipleship teaching that the church has neglected for many decades. This insightful book answers the questions that many young adults are asking about Christianity. Topics like the person of Jesus, the Bible, the new birth, the Holy Spirit, and much more make this book a valuable tool for any church seeking to make disciples.

Reasons for Believing points the reader to the foundational truths the church desperately needs to understand once again. The book makes it clear that discipleship must, once again, become a significant element in the Body of Christ, the church.

J. Steve Sells, *President*
Operation Transformation

Preface

As this book goes to press a news story is on the airways that shares the account of a little 7th Grade girl in Katy, Texas who related to the local School Board her unhappy and trying experience in the public school classroom when she felt that her faith was under attack. Her testimony was, "Today I was given an assignment in school that questioned my faith and told me that God was not real. Our teacher had started the class by saying that the assignment had been giving problems all day. We were asked to take a Poll to say whether God is fact, opinion, or a myth and she told everyone who said fact or opinion was wrong and God was only a myth." The news account, written by Victor Skinner and carried by **Common Core Watch**, stated that the teen had spoken to other students in the class who were "marked down" because of their belief that God is real as well as compromises by some students to avoid rejecting their faith.

This is not an isolated case. There are similar reports coming from all parts of the Country as well as from college campuses where Christians are often ostracized and criticized for their Christian faith. It is shocking to millions of Americans to learn that this kind of thing is happening in America where the First Amendment guarantees that, "Congress shall make no law respecting the establishment of religion, **or prohibiting the free exercise thereof** ..." Marxists have invaded not only the High Schools of America but the college campuses as well and they peddle their anti-God fanaticism without restraint.

It is the purpose of this book to provide an opportunity for young adults in High School, College, and their family members the tools to explain the very basic teachings of Christianity as well as to present the Biblical teachings of their faith.

This is not a fast-read book. It is a study book. The reader of this book should keep the Bible handy because there are numerous Scriptural references that should command a vigorous contextual examination for a thorough understanding of the basic beliefs of the Christian faith so that the believer will *"...be ready always to give an answer to every man that asketh you a reason for the hope that is in you."* (I Peter 3: 15) The reader who will master the materials herein will be equipped to disciple other believers who face constant questions and even attacks concerning their faith in Jesus Christ. This book is written with a prayer that it will provide the basis for a great Christian renewal among the young adults of America.

It is the position of this book that the Bible is the inerrant **Word of God** and is the most perfect and reliable source of historical events that exist. While it is a book of revelation and not science, it is totally trustworthy where it touches scientific matters such as creation. It is a perfect treasure of Divine truth and contains no error. It is the author's belief that *"all Scripture is given by inspiration of God, and is profitable for doctrine, for reproof, for correction, for instruction in righteousness that the man of God may be complete, thoroughly furnished unto all good works."* (II Timothy 3: 16-17)

Introduction

Young Adults have some nagging but honest questions about the Christian faith. The Scriptures, however, always have an answer because they have an eternal nature about them. In the early days of America, Deism was sweeping over the pulpits of this nation and drying up the churches but God raised up some men like George Whitfield, the Wesley brothers, Jonathan Edwards and others who were mightily used in the First and Second Great Awakenings. They passionately preached the Word of God because they knew that **the Scriptures had the answer.**

Today, Christianity, again, faces some unusually debilitating problems. Even secular TV Commentators state clearly that Christianity is under attack. Christian institutions are being ordered by government to fund birth control to students and patients. Homosexual teachings are being forced upon children as early as second grade among other things. Again, the **Scriptures** give us the answer. Our problems are many and devastating. It is the purpose of this book to delve into the Scriptures because they speak so **clearly** and **pungently** to the problems that young adults face in this hour. We must also point out the teachings of corresponding Scripture.

The Johannine literature (scripture written by the Apostle John) is a precious treasure for all Christians. We rely on it heavily in this book for a reason. It expands our minds and feeds our souls. Often copies of the **Gospel of John** are printed and distributed when there are not enough resources to distribute the entire Bible. It is because we understand the nature of John's writings so well. There is always a Godly appeal in them. Of course, the Johannine literature includes the Gospel of John as well as the three letters of John plus the Revelation. Christians will find edification and enlightenment in all of his writings. Many other Scriptures, however, are employed to support the theses of this book.

John was the brother of James and Zebedee was their father. Their mother was Salome who was the sister of Mary, the mother of Jesus. There is little doubt about that kinship. This means that they were cousins of Jesus after the flesh. Of course, God was the Father of Jesus. That is the meaning of the virgin birth. Zebedee and his two sons were apparently partners in the fishing business with Peter and Andrew (Matthew 27: 56; Mark 16:1). Apparently, they were affluent enough that they were able to have hired servants (Mark 1: 19-20; Luke 5: 7-10). When John answered the call of Jesus to be one of his disciples, he gave our Lord **absolute** and **complete** devotion. Yes, they did have some problems. Jesus gave the brothers the name of Boanerges, which means "Sons of Thunder." They could sometimes be petulant (Mark 9:38; Luke 9:49).

John, we learn from his writings, was very close to Jesus. At the Last Supper, John laid his head on the shoulder of Jesus in his grief. Even though the brothers of Jesus were still living (James, Joses, Simon and Jude) He committed the care of His own mother to John who stood right there at the foot of the cross in loyalty to Christ while the other disciples had quietly slipped away (John 19: 25 - 27).

There is something unusual here. This disciple who had such an impetuous, explosive personality when he was young **would not even mention his own name** when he came to write his gospel about 95 AD. He simply referred to himself as *"that disciple whom Jesus loved."* That was **all that mattered to him** then. No one, however, should mistake his mellowness with willingness to compromise because there was no compromise in him. Irenaeus, an early church theologian and historian, related a story that took place when John was pastor of the large church in Ephesus. There was a Gnostic heretic there by the name of Cerinthus. Gnostics believed in a perverse kind of salvation through knowledge irrespective of Jesus. John would not even talk with Cerinthus. When Cerinthus joined a group, of which John was a part John would immediately leave the group because he so much detested the heresy of Cerinthus. He could not bear to remain under the same roof with him. Once, when he learned that Cerinthus was in the bathhouse, John cried out *"Let us flee lest the bath fall, for Cerinthus, the enemy of the truth is within."* Eusebius who was an early church pastor and historian confirmed this story.

Jerome, famous for his translation of the scriptures into Latin, tells of the last words of John as he lay dying. Some of his followers asked if he had a message for them. His message was, *"Little children, love one another."* He repeated it over and over and as he passed from this life he said, *"It is the Lord's command."* It is John who is named as the beloved disciple (John 13: 23 - 33; 19: 25 - 27; 20: 2; 21:20; 19: 34-35). It is this John that we look to during these troubled times to expand our minds and feed our souls on manna from Heaven. When the truth concerning Christ was on the line, John would strike no compromise or yield any quarter. Perhaps that is the reason that Jesus placed so much trust in John. It is this John who, writing under the inspiration of the Holy Spirit, speaks to the kinds of problems that plague young Americans today. He gives us answers to which we can tie. In this book, we also reference corresponding and supporting Scriptures so that the reader will grasp the pervasiveness of these truths throughout the Scripture.

We have also looked to the writings of the great Apostle Paul; the physician, Luke; young Mark; the great leaders of the early Christian Church, Peter and Matthew, the writer of the first book of the New Testament. Yet, who could ignore the practical letter of James, the earthly brother of Jesus as well as another younger brother of Jesus whom we know as Jude.

It is our hope and prayer that the reader will read this book with an open mind giving particular attention to the Scriptures cited in these writings. If one believes in the authority of Scripture, there is help and understanding in these pages; if not, there is neither help nor hope from any other source.

Chapter One
Is Jesus Real?

In today's world, many questions are being raised about the reality of Jesus Christ. Is He authentic? Is He genuine and indisputable? Is He who He claims to be? Is He really the personification of truth? Is He really a part of the Holy Trinity and does He have power? Did He really secure eternal life for those who believe? Does He really have the power that He claimed before He ascended from this earth? Many people, young and old, have these questions swirling in their minds and hearts. They have doubts. They do not know. Sometimes they hear His name denigrated and disparaged in the classroom. Sadly enough, they sometimes hear His name sullied by teachers in the religious world and even from pulpits. It is often that young and old alike ask the question, "Is there a sure and certain word concerning Jesus?" The Answer Is "Yes"

The answer is "Yes." A thousand times, "Yes." Cynics have always attacked the person of Jesus Christ. Throughout history, Jesus has been a polarizing figure. It is not that Jesus wanted it that way but Jesus came into a fallen world that was depraved because of sin and disobedience. It was true in John's day. It is true today.

Most of the atrocious and heinous heresies of Christianity have revolved around the two natures of Christ. All of them were terribly destructive. As is usually the case, most destructive heresies of Christianity have always started with pseudo-scholars. The earliest heresies came from Gnosticism, which springs from the Greek root word ginosko (γινωσκω) which simply means, "To come to know." It grew from some self-styled scholars who thought they understood things they did not understand. Gnosticism held that all matter is evil and that God could not have dwelt in a human body. Gnosticism took several forms. There were not only the Docetics, but also Ebionism, which denied Christ's full deity. The Docetics argued that Jesus only appeared to have a body but was really an apparition or a phantom type being. They contended, for instance, that Jesus left no tracks in the dust when He walked along the road and if one tried to touch Him, He was not there. Some referred to this as "seemism". We will discuss more about this later. Cerinthus of Ephesus, who was a vile and vicious opponent of John, taught that divinity came upon Christ at His baptism but departed from Him before the Crucifixion. Most of the heresies attack the reality of Jesus Christ as the God/Man. The attacks may come under different headings but they are basically the same heresies that have dogged the steps of Christianity through the centuries.

John's Answer

John has an answer as to the reality and nature of Jesus Christ. In John 1: 1, the Apostle refers to Jesus as the "**Word.**" In John's culture, **words** did things. They were **powerful** and the same is true today.

The iconic actor, John Wayne, was once playing the role of a Texas Ranger. A riverboat gambler/murderer that he had arrested was trying to persuade Wayne to let him go. Wayne told him that he could not let him go. The gambler/murderer did not understand why. Wayne said, "It is because of the oath I took." The gambler said, "Just words." The reply of Wayne was a classic. He said, "Words are what men live by." Nations are founded by words that men believe and live by. Our nation was founded upon a Constitution. Yes, the Constitution is made up of words. We have a Supreme Court to enforce the Constitution. The Declaration of

Independence declares that all men are created equally and that we have "inalienable rights, among which are life, liberty and the pursuit of happiness." Those are words that people live by. Homes are founded upon words. A man and woman stand before a pastor and enter into vows by which they live their lives together. Property is held by words. If one has a warranty deed then he has possession of the house in which he lives and the land on which it is located.

Communication

Words form our communication. Without communication, we would live in chaos. **Jesus** was **God's ultimate communication** with man. He is God's ultimate **Word**! John is making that clear. John records the word of Jesus to that effect when He said, "*...he who has seen me has seen the Father so how can you say, **show me the Father**?*" (John 14: 9b) Again, Jesus said, "*Believe me that **I am in the Father and the Father in me** ...*" (John 14: 11a)

What Is God Like?

Therefore, John makes it clear for all the doubters and naysayers about the reality of Jesus. **Jesus** was the **Word**. He was the ultimate revelation of God to man. If we want to know what God is like, we simply look at Jesus. When did the Word first exist? It was "*in the beginning.*" This tells us that Jesus was a part of the **Godhead**. He was a part of the **Trinity** and was active in **Creation**. For all who would doubt the divinity of Christ, the Apostle John makes it clear. He was **with God** in the **Beginning**. He is **eternal** and He **is** a part of the Godhead. This is the John who was with Him throughout His ministry on earth. Since he was His cousin, he would know about the **virgin birth** of Christ. He knew all there was to know about Christ who became flesh and walked on the earth. This is not a man who theorized about Christ. This is not one who sat with philosophers or teachers to speculate about **who** Jesus was. This is that "***disciple whom Jesus loved***" and who travelled with Him during His sojourn on earth. These words did not come from the pen of a novice but from the pen of a veteran who stood by Jesus right on up to the end on Calvary's Hill.

To those who would doubt that Jesus was the God/Man, John gives a certain answer. In the first epistle of John he faithfully declares, "*That which was from the **Beginning** which we have* **heard.** *Which we have seen with our eyes, which we have looked upon, and our hands have handled concerning the word of life...*" (I John 1: 1-2) With these words, John curtly dismisses the claims of the Docetics that Jesus was an apparition or a phantom. John makes it known that they looked upon Him and they touched Him. They also heard Him speak. John clearly affirms that Jesus was as much **God** as He was **man** and as much man as He was God. In verse 3 John goes over it again as though to reiterate and burnish into our minds what he has said about the life that was manifested through Christ saying: "*That which we have seen and heard we declare to you, that you may also have fellowship with us; and truly our fellowship is with the Father and with His Son Jesus Christ. And these things we write to you that your joy may be full.*" (I John 1: 3-4).

The Clincher

Probably the most deleterious blow that John struck against insipid and malignant Docetic Gnosticism is found in John 1: 14 as John begins to wind down the prologue. Not only has he stated that Jesus is the **Word** who is eternal and was with God in the Beginning but that the **Word became flesh** and **dwelt** among us. John is clearly establishing the fact that God did not simply become man at Bethlehem but that He became the **God/Man** when He was incarnated into the flesh. The word that is translated "dwelt" is **eskenosen** (εσκηνοσην). It means that "He pitched His tent" among us or that he "tabernacled" among us. The Apostle Paul, who saw John as one of the pillars of the church, (Galatians 2: 9) speaks of our physical bodies as *"our earthly house of this* **tabernacle***."* Again, he points out that *"We that are in this* **tabernacle** *do groan, being burdened; not for that we would be unclothed but clothed upon that mortality might be swallowed up of life."* (II Corinthians 5: 1-4). In this, Paul declares that Christ not only was **divine** but that He was also **human**. Indeed, He was the **God/Man**.

However, John does not let up. Not only did the **Word** become flesh and dwell among us; but also John declares emphatically that he witnessed it all when he said, *"We* **beheld** *His* **glory***, the glory as of the only begotten of the Father,* **full of grace and truth***."* Truth informs us concerning the way of salvation and God extends salvation to us by His grace. John makes it clear that John the Baptist also bore witness of this fact (John 1:15). Since John's Mother and Mary the Mother of Jesus were sisters, John the Baptist was John's relative also as his Mother (Elizabeth) was a cousin to Mary and Salome.

What are we to take from those powerful words of John when he said; *"We beheld His glory"?* John is testifying that he witnessed the **glory** of **God**. This, more than anything else, presents Jesus Christ as that only begotten Son of God. This mention of the glory surrounding Jesus Christ harks back to the **Shekinah** glory that abode upon Mount Sinai at the giving of the Ten Commandments. The Bible tells us that God's glory rested upon Mount Sinai in the form of a **cloud** and that the cloud covered the Mountain for 6 days. The glory of the Lord has been described on that occasion as being like a consuming fire. Moses went into the midst of the cloud and stayed for 40 days and nights at which time he received the instructions for the building of the tabernacle as well as the reconstruction of the Ark of the Covenant and the Ten

Commandments (Exodus 24: 16-18). When things looked so helpless and futile to the Children of Israel they looked toward the desert and saw the glory of God in the form of a cloud. They were facing starvation and the Lord provided quails for them in the evening and manna in the mornings (Exodus 16: 10 - 15). When the tabernacle was erected, the **cloud** of **God's glory** filled the tabernacle and it became known as *"the tent of meeting"* because that is where the people went to commune with God. As the people journeyed they were guided by the cloud of God's glory by day and a pillar of fire by night and the glory of God stayed with them throughout their journeys (Exodus 40: 34-38).

In His Ministry

The glory of God attended the works of Jesus on earth and John is making sure that everyone understands that because nothing is more real concerning Christ than the glory of God that rested upon Him.

The glory of God was attendant at His first miracle in Cana of Galilee where he turned water into wine. The Scriptures tell us that, during that miracle, the glory of God was manifested and His disciples believed in Him (John 2:11).

The Scriptures are clear that the glory manifested by Jesus was not a glory that He sought for Himself but He made it clear that His glory came from God and it was God's glory that was being manifested through Him. He said clearly that, *"he who speaks from himself seeks his own glory; but he who seeks the **glory** of the one who sent him is **true**, and no unrighteousness is in him"* (John 7:18). Jesus assured His followers that, *"The Son of Man will come in the **glory** of His Father with His angels, and then He will reward each according to his works"* (Matthew 16:28). Six days after that statement Jesus took Peter, James, and John up on a high mountain (believed to be Mount Tabor, which has an elevation of more than 1,800 feet). While they were on the Mount, the disciples saw Jesus transfigured before their eyes. His face did shine like the sun and His clothes were as white as the light. Moses who had experienced the glory of God atop Sinai and Elijah who had experienced the glory of God atop Mount Carmel met Jesus there. In Luke's account he tells us that Moses and Elijah *"appeared in glory and spoke of His decease which He was about to accomplish at Jerusalem"* (Luke 9: 28-31). Luke also points out that when the disciples were fully awake, *"They saw **His glory.**"* The word that is translated "decease" is from the Greek word exodon (ἔξοδον) from which our word exodus is derived. It refers to a departure. He was talking to Moses and Elijah. Moses had led the Children of Israel out of the bondage of Egypt. Elijah had led them out of the bondage of Baalism and at Calvary Jesus would lead the world out of the bondage of sin. There, on that mountaintop, Jesus and the disciples witnessed again the glory of God who descended in a bright cloud and surrounded them.

Peter's Attempt

Peter had been attempting to dissuade Jesus from Jerusalem and the cross (Matthew 16: 22-23). It was only a few days later that they were on the Mount of Transfiguration. When Peter saw the radiance of Jesus' face and the glistening of His garments as He talked with heavenly visitors, Peter tried again. He wanted to build three tabernacles atop that mountain: one would be for Jesus, one would be for Moses, and one would be for Elijah. It is at that point that the **glory** of the cloud engulfed them and God spoke. It is **hard to escape** the belief that God was addressing Peter at this time as He said, *"This is my beloved Son, in whom I am well pleased. **Hear Him**"!* Peter was saying, "Let's build three tabernacles here and forget about Jerusalem and the cross that you have been talking about." God was saying, "Peter, this is my

11

beloved Son. I am well pleased with the way that He is obeying me. You listen to Him. He says Jerusalem and the cross. That's the way it has to be." (See Matthew 17: 1-9)

There were many other times when John had witnessed the glory of God attending the ministry of Jesus. He had seen it at the resurrection of Lazarus (John 11: 4 & 40). The glory of God was manifested in the resurrection of Christ (Romans 6:4). He was also glorified in His ascension and exaltation (I Peter 1: 21). Peter also recorded the **"excellent glory"** which was revealed on the mountaintop (II Peter 1: 17-18). The word **glory** is translated from the Greek word doxa (δοξα), from which we get our word, doxology. It refers to the nature and acts of God in self-manifestation, in regard to who He essentially is and what He does. That is particularly done in the person and work of Jesus Christ our Lord (John 17: 5 & 24). John witnessed it all. When John says that he "*beheld*" His glory he used the word theaomai (Θεαομαι). It means to view attentively, contemplatively, with a sense of awe and wonder. John has no doubt and he was there. Jesus was very real to him.

The One and Only

When John beheld Christ's glory, it was not just a single occasion. He had seen him perform miracles. He witnessed Jesus raise Lazarus from the dead. He witnessed Jesus raising the son of the widow of Nain. He witnessed Him calm the sea. He made the lame to walk, the blind to see and the deaf to hear. What was John's conclusion? He saw the glory of God attending all of those great miracles and he concluded that Jesus was "*the only begotten of the Father, full of grace and truth.*" The Greek word he uses for "the only begotten" was "monogenous" (μονογηνους). This term is used 5 times in the New Testament and all of them are in the writings of the Apostle John. It can be translated as the "one and only" or "the unique one" or "one of a kind". John leaves no doubt that Jesus is the real God/Man. In fact, John made that clear when he said, *"every spirit that **does not confess** that Jesus Christ has come in the **flesh** is not of God. And this is the spirit of the antichrist, which you have heard was coming, and now is already in the world"* (I John 4: 3-4). This is the most severe blow to the Docetics. It comes from the Greek word *"**dokein**"* (δοκειν). It means, "To seem to be." The Docetics embraced a heresy that was particularly debilitating to the church and to the spread of the Gospel. They believed that Jesus could not suffer pain. They believed that He could not suffer sorrow. They believed that when He walked He did not leave tracks in the dust because He was not real. They did not believe that He could feel hunger or weariness. They believed that He could not suffer anger, fear, or grief according to the heretics. Of course, such nonsense would negate that great 53rd Chapter of Isaiah, especially verses 4 and 5 which declares to us that *"surely He hath bourn our griefs and carried our sorrows: yet we did esteem Him stricken, smitten of God, and afflicted. He was wounded for our transgressions, He was bruised for our iniquities: the chastisement of our peace was upon Him; and with His stripes we are healed"* (Isaiah 53: 4 & 5 KJV). It would also negate many other prophesies concerning our Lord. John, however, would have none of it. He was never willing to sit down with heretics and try to "come to an understanding" or "find points of agreement." **He believed in a pure Gospel.** He was the one who recorded the words of Jesus when Jesus declared that, *"I am the way, the truth, and the life. No one comes to the Father except through me"* (John 14: 6). The mind of the natural man staggers at this. This is what Paul is saying to the Corinthians when he points out that *"the natural man does not receive the things of the spirit of God, for they are foolishness to him; nor can he know them, because they are **spiritually discerned.**"* (I Corinthians 2: 14).

13

Grace and Truth

Not only did John understand that Jesus was the "**God/Man**" but He was full of **grace** and **truth**. The word **grace** is translated from the Greek word charis (χαρις). The term is all encompassing. It refers to a character trait in which one is courteous, caring, proper, and kind. It refers to an attitude reflected in speech. It refers to a friendly disposition from which kind acts proceed. It bespeaks of good will and divine favor. The grace of God can never be earned, purchased, or deserved. It describes God's redemptive mercy and the pleasure or the joy that God extends to the recipient. John makes it clear that the grace of God extends far beyond any grace that is offered through the law and Jesus is the personification of God's grace. When Christ died for sinful men, it was not anything that man deserved. It was purely an act of God's love. It magnifies the helplessness of man to save himself and the boundless love of God to extend salvation to those who did not deserve it. That was God's boundless grace in action!

Divine Embodiment

Because of the divine embodiment of grace in Jesus Christ the Lord, multitudes followed Him and hung on His every word. It manifested the power of God to save man from the presence, penalty, and power of sin.

When Peter drew his sword in the Garden of Gethsemane and slashed off the ear of the Centurion's servant, Jesus exemplified the grace of God so that any man could understand it. He told Peter to put up his sword because a loving God did not need it. He reminded Peter that He could call down 12 legions of angels who could have obliterated every enemy in Jerusalem but that kind of act would be diametrically opposed to the Lord's mission on earth. He then healed the servant's ear. **What a Savior!** If any reader needs more demonstration of the reality of Christ, there is more,

Truth is the second consuming word in this passage. It is one of John's dominant notes. The personhood of Jesus is the embodiment of truth. If we want to know what truth is, we simply look to Jesus. Sometimes vain men draw strange, ungodly notions and pen ridiculous, truncated, and heretical prose about the Savior that is inimical to the spread of the Gospel and impugns the very nature and love of God. They defend such repulsive activities as being a search for **truth.** That is, however, a fallacious claim because Jesus has made it clear that He is the *"way, the **truth** and the life."* If we want to see and know what truth is we simply look at Jesus and His life. John has definite instructions to the believer who faces those who deny the doctrine of Jesus Christ as it is taught in the Scripture. His instruction is that, *"if anyone comes to you and does not bring this doctrine, do not receive him into your house nor greet him; for he who greets him shares in his evil deeds"* (II John 10 & 11). This serves as a warning that there are those heretics who would diminish the Gospel of the Son of God, who would seek to come into the Christian fellowship and bring confusion and division. John is aware that believers have a tendency to be courteous and to listen to anyone who comes among them. Such an attitude can be destructive to their faith. He leaves no doubt that they are to be firmly rejected and that the believer is not to give them any kind of recommendation to any other group. If any man is in search of the truth, he simply needs to look to the Scripture and read everything he can about Jesus because Jesus is not an abstract idea. He is a **reality**. He is the **truth**.

Men for centuries had been trying to understand and define God but when Jesus came into the world, they saw a perfect picture, a **divine definition**, of God. We can always look at Jesus Christ and say, "that is what God is like." Jesus did not walk on earth to philosophize about God. Jesus made it clear to Phillip that "He *who has seen me has seen the Father*" (John 14:9). His challenge to His disciples was, "*believe me that I am in the Father and the Father in me, or else **believe me for the sake of the works themselves***" (John 13: 11). In fact, Jesus made it clear on many occasions that He performed the miracles that He performed in order to authenticate the message He was delivering. His miracles were not the work of prestidigitation (sleight of hand) as some would have you believe but He actually suspended the laws of nature to demonstrate His power and His authority from **Heaven**. We saw it when he calmed the sea, healed the demoniac, and raised Lazarus from the dead as well as other miraculous works or, what some would call, **mighty works**. In Jesus, we observe God living His life in the form of a man and showing us, by example, how God would have us live, and we are never more Godly than when we are following the example of Jesus. This tells us that **Jesus is the ultimate reality!**

We Receive of Him

Not only is Christ full of **grace** and **truth** but John makes it clear that all God has is available to us. He declared "*... of His fullness we have all received and **grace for grace**.*" Here we see the power and ministry of the **indwelling Christ**. It is a powerful truth so wonderful that it is difficult for the human mind and heart to conceive of it or fathom it; to know that the Creator of this universe; the one who put the stars in place and who turns the earth on its' axis; the one who created all the beauty of nature; is the one who loves us enough to have **suffered** for us on **Calvary**! That is the kind of mighty power that works on our behalf throughout our Christian walk. What does that term "grace for grace" really mean? It means that every grace that we receive is ultimately replaced by grace that is greater and more beautiful. It is like driving along the beautiful Blue Ridge Parkway in North Carolina. One can stop at an Overlook and look out across the vast valleys that are breathless in their beauty. One can stand there and declare that he will never see a picture more beautiful; but he can go on up the Parkway, see another beautiful scene even more beautiful than the one he left behind, and know that it is the handiwork of God. That is the way it is when we walk with Christ dwelling within us. As children, we sang a little children's song that said it all:

"Every day with Jesus
Is sweeter than the day before.
Every day with Jesus
I love Him more and more.
Jesus saves and keeps me
And He is the one I'm living for.
Every day with Jesus
Is sweeter than the day before."

Paul understood this when he described the pre-eminence of Christ in his letter to the Colossians as he pointed out that, "by Him were all things created that are in heaven and that are on earth, visible and invisible, whether thrones or dominions or principalities or powers. All things were created through Him and for Him and He is before all things, and in Him all things consist. And He is the head of the body, the church, who is the beginning, the firstborn from the dead, that in all things He may have the pre-eminence" (Colossians 1: 15-18). He is speaking of that same pre-eminent Christ when he pointed out that "it pleased the Father that in Him **all the fullness** should dwell." (Verse 19)

The longer we know Christ the more wonderful He becomes. The more we pray in His name, the more we understand Him. The more we look for His mighty works all around us, the more love we discover. It means that God has a grace to cover every situation. When we are successful one kind of grace is required.

When we suffer failure, another kind of grace is required. When we are well and healthy, we experience one kind of grace but when we are sick and suffering, He provides another kind of grace that gives us comfort. He did not promise to keep us out of the storms of life but He promised to walk through them with us. Jesus could have **prevented** the **storm** on the **Sea of Galilee** but instead He saw them through it (John 6: 15 - 21). Jesus compared Himself to the vine and we are the branches. He points out that every vine that does not bear fruit will be cut away but even that vine that bears fruit will be **pruned**. Pruning involves **cutting**. It involves some **pain**. A person who has an apple orchard or a vineyard knows how important pruning is. He knows that if the tree or vine is not pruned, it will soon cease to bear good fruit because the fruit comes on the **new growth**. The pruning is so that the tree or the vine will **bear more fruit.** (John 15: 1-2) Sometimes, when the Lord does pruning in our lives, it is painful but He lets it happen because through that experience we learn to **bear more fruit!** John is pressing that truth home. The more we **know** about **Christ** and His teachings the more **wonderful** He becomes. The more we think of Him the better we understand Him. The longer we live with Him the more lovely He becomes and the more lovable we become. We may need one kind of grace in the rising sun of our youth and a different kind of grace in the evening of our lives. It is much like the sun. The sun rises in the morning and shines brightly all the day, but the most **beautiful time** is at sunset. That is what people love to see - the **beauty** of the **sunset**. That is the way it is in our lives. The most **beautiful** days of your life may be the **sun setting** days of your life. In those days when you need courage, God will provide that courage through His Son. During those days when you are **persecuted** for His name's sake, you need **grace** and it is a different kind of grace than you need when you succeed. It takes one kind of grace when you are **happy** and things are going well in your life but it takes another kind of grace when you are living in difficult days. Through Christ, we are no longer **slaves** of sin but sons and heirs of God. When needs arise in our lives our Lord has a grace to cover them and it is only through Jesus Christ that we have *"the right to become children of God, to those who believe in His name."* (John 1: 12)

The Miracles of Jesus

One of the most persuasive elements of Jesus' ministry was the **miracles** or the **great works** that he performed. As referred to earlier, Jesus made it clear that these miracles were performed in order that men might **believe** that He was the Son of God and the Savior of the World. At the **first miracle** in Cana of Galilee John recorded that *"it manifested His glory; and **His disciples believed in Him**"* (John 2: 11). The Greek word for believe is **pisteuo** (πιστευω). John uses the word 84 times in his Gospel and 5 times in his first epistle. The basic meaning of the term is "to **trust** or rely upon." Believing on the Lord Jesus was a recurring theme in John's Gospel. The **second great work** came after Jesus had been to Jerusalem and returned to Galilee. He was again in the city of Cana where His first miracle was performed. A nobleman approached Him who had a son in the process of dying. Jesus told him to go his way and his son would live. When the nobleman asked Jesus to come down to His house and heal his child Jesus clearly stated to him, *"Unless you people see **signs** and **wonders**, you will by no means **believe**"* (John 4: 48). On his way home his servants met him and assured him that his son would live. His fever had broken. When they gave him the time of the boy's healing, he remembered that it was the very hour in which Jesus had assured him that the boy would live and the nobleman **believed.**

The **third sign** or **miracle** was done at the Pool of Bethesda. There was a lame man who lay beside the pool. Jesus healed him.

After the performance of that sign or miracle, the Jews sought to slay Jesus (John 5: 16). Their persecution of Jesus became more intense when He informed them that God was His father making Him equal with God. It was on that occasion that Jesus announced that *"He who hears My word and **believes** in Him who sent Me has everlasting life, and shall not come into condemnation, but is past from death into life."* (John 5: 24) On that same occasion, Jesus said, *"The works which the Father hath given me to finish - **the very works that I do** - bear witness of Me, that the Father hath sent me"* (verse 36). He makes it clear that the mighty works, which He is doing, are for the specific purpose of bearing witness of the fact that the Father had sent Him. Unless we see Christ as the **Son of God** and a part of the **Godhead**, whatever else we think does not matter. This simply underscores what John has already told us that *"when He was in Jerusalem at the Passover, during the Feast, many **believed** in His name when they saw the **signs** which He did."* Again, John gives us the purpose of the mighty signs and wonders.

The **fourth great sign** is the feeding of the five thousand. When the great multitude was coming toward Jesus, His disciples were exasperated because they did not understand how they could possibly feed them all (John 6: 5). When Jesus had them to sit down by companies, He took five barley loaves and two fish and multiplied them so that everyone was filled and there were twelve baskets left over. When the people saw it they said, *"This truly is the **prophet** who is to come into the world"* (John 6: 14). It is obvious that they **believed.**

The **fifth great sign** was that of Jesus walking on the water. After the feeding of the five thousand, Jesus perceived that they were going to take Him by force and make him king which would have **hindered** His purpose for coming into the world. He then departed again to a mountain by Himself alone. In the meantime, His disciples went down to the sea and took a boat to go over to Capernaum. Jesus had not come with them. There was a great wind that bore down upon them and the sea became boisterous. After they had rowed about 3 or 4 miles, they saw Jesus walking on the sea and they were afraid. He comforted them by saying, *"It is I; do not be afraid."* Many of the people went around the edge of the sea to Capernaum and saw Jesus. They knew He did not go with the disciples and that there was no other way He could have arrived there. When they asked Him how He got there, He warned them that they were not seeking Him because of the **great signs** but because they were **filled** with the **food**. He cautioned them not to labor for the food that would perish but for the **food**, which **endures** to **everlasting life**. When they inquired of Him as to what they might do to work the works of God, Jesus said to them, *"This is the work of God, that you **believe** in Him whom He sent"* (John 6: 29). Again, we see His purpose in performing the great miracles and that purpose was that the people might **believe**. On one occasion Jesus even said, *"If I do not do the works of My Father, do not **believe Me**; but if I do, though you do not **believe** Me, **believe** the works, that you may know and **believe** that the Father is in Me and I in Him"* (John 10: 37 - 38). There we have the **basic reason** stated again for the **great signs and wonders** that Jesus performed on earth.

The **sixth great sign** or **miracle** was that of restoring sight to a blind man (John 9: 1-41). This miracle comes after Jesus had established His eternal nature with the Father. The Jews accused Him of having a devil but Jesus replied, *"Your Father **Abraham** rejoiced to **see My day**: and he **saw it**, and was **glad"**.* It was immediately after this encounter that He uttered that famous phrase: *"Before Abraham was, **I am.**"* This harks back to Exodus 3: 14 where this term refers to the person of God. Jesus is asserting His existence with God even before Abraham was born. It is also quite possible that Abraham saw Jesus when he met Melchizedek upon his return from the battle where he rescued his nephew, Lot. Melchizedek was an Old Testament manifestation of Christ. (Genesis 14: 18-20; Hebrews 7: 1-3) The

21

Heavenly Father was known as the **Great I Am.** At this point the Jews were so incited to kill that they took up stones and Jesus disappeared from their midst. It was after this that Jesus passed by and saw a man blind from his birth. His disciples inquired, *"Who sinned, this man or his parents, that he was born blind?"* Jesus' answer was that, *"neither this man nor his parents sinned, but that the **works of God** should be revealed in Him."* (John 9: 3-4) Jesus made spittle of clay and placed it on his eyes. He then required something of obedience for the man to receive his sight. Because the man believed he went down to the Pool of Siloam, according to the instructions of Jesus, where he washed his eyes and received his sight. When Jesus saw him later He said, *"Do you **believe** in the **Son of God?**"* This tells us that God had a purpose in the life of this man even from the time he was born and that purpose was that not only this man, but also thousands and millions of others who would read about this incident would believe on the name of Jesus.

Raising of Lazarus

Now we come to the **seventh sign,** which towers over all the other miracles Jesus performed. It is the raising of Lazarus. (John 11: 1-45) Jesus had been to Jerusalem for the Feast of Dedication. Opposition erupted because of Jesus' teachings concerning His relationship to the Father. The Pharisees, when they heard Jesus say, *"The Father is in Me, and I in Him"* (John 10:38), sought to seize Him but He escaped from their hands and went beyond Jordan to the place where John was baptizing in the early part of His ministry. Many in that area came to hear Him and **believed** on Him. Back at Bethany, **Lazarus,** the brother of Mary and Martha, became severely ill. His sisters sent for Jesus. When Jesus received the news, He stayed two more days in the place where He was. He informed His disciples that Lazarus was dead and called upon them to go back to Judea with Him. They were afraid to go because the people in Judea had lately sought to stone Jesus to death. After Jesus informed them of Lazarus' death He said, *"And I am glad for **your sakes** that I was not there, **that you may believe**. Nevertheless, let us go to him."* In exasperation, Thomas said, *"Let us also go, that we die with Him."* When Martha received the news that Jesus was on His way she ran to meet Him. She seemed to be a bit miffed. She told Him that if He had been there her brother would not have died but even then, she knew that *"**whatever** you ask of **God**, God will give you."* (Verse 22) Jesus assured her that her brother would live again. She thought that Jesus was talking about the final resurrection in the last day but Jesus said to her, *"I am the **resurrection** and **the life**. He who **believes** in Me, though he may die, he shall live."* (Verse 25) He again assures her that, *"Whoever lives and believes in Me shall never die. Do you **believe** this?"* When they came to the tomb and Jesus asked Martha to take away the stone, she was afraid that he smelled. Then Jesus again underscores the nature of belief when He said, *"Did not I say to you that if you would **believe** you would see the **glory of God**?"* There is that word **glory** again! Through his death and resuscitation, Lazarus glorified God. After Jesus had prayed to the Father, He called Lazarus forth out of the grave and Lazarus came forth. Jesus' final word on the matter was, *"Loose him and let him go."* What was the result? We find it in Verse 45 when John points out that, *"Many of the Jews who had come to Mary, and had seen the things Jesus did, **believed** in Him."*

Of course, Jesus did many other miracles such as the draught of fish and the raising of the son of a widow in Nain but John has selected these mighty works that we have discussed here in order to illustrate the reason for Jesus' miracles. It was that men might **believe** and that God would be **glorified**.

The Resurrection

The very **pinnacle** of evidence regarding the **reality** of Jesus Christ is the Resurrection. The certainty of Christianity rests upon its great truths and the greatest of these is the **bodily resurrection of Jesus Christ from the grave**. Christianity has a truth that no other religion in the entire universe can claim. The tomb of Lennon is **occupied**. The tomb of Mohammed is **occupied**. The tomb of Buddha is **occupied** but the tomb of Jesus Christ, the Son of God is **empty**. All of the Gospel writers bear **testimony** to the **resurrection** of **Jesus Christ** from the **grave**. The Apostle John gives us an account that is especially heartwarming, comforting, and assuring to every believer in Christ because he answers the basic question of any religion. That question is whether or not anyone has cheated death. Has anyone **conquered** the **last enemy**? The answer to that is a resounding, "**Yes**."

John does not sugar coat his account of the Resurrection. **It did not come easy to some of His disciples**. The idea was so ingrained in the Jewish culture that the Messiah would come, raising mighty armies and conquer all the armies of Israel's earthly enemies that it was hard for them to believe anything else. The Priests, the Pharisees, the Sadducees, and the Scribes (the intellectuals of Israel); at least those who held high office in **organized religion**, were never convinced. There were a few exceptions such as Nicodemus, but for the most part, they were the ones who called for His **crucifixion**! Yes, Jesus had warned His disciples at Caesarea Philippi that He must go up to Jerusalem and that He would suffer many things at the hands of the **Elders**, the **Chief Priests** and the **Scribes**; that He would be killed and be raised again the third day. (Matthew 16:21) Even Peter had a difficult time accepting that even though he had just confessed that Jesus was the **Christ**, the **Son of the living God**. (Verses 22 &

23) Jesus had told the multitudes that He was the Son of God. Once, at the Feast of Dedication in Jerusalem, Jesus walked onto Solomon's Porch. The Jews gathered around Him asking Him to declare Himself as to whether or not He was the **Son of God** or the **Christ**. Jesus reminded them of the mighty works that He had done in His Father's name. He said to them that those works would bear **witness** of Him. It was on that occasion that Jesus said, *"I and My Father are one."* (John 10:30) The response was that they took up stones to stone Him. He again pointed out to them the **mighty** works that He had done and challenged them to **believe for the sake of the mighty works** (Verses 37 & 38). The answer from the crowd was that they sought again to stone Him and He left to go beyond Jordan. Even Martha, the sister of Lazarus whom Jesus raised up, found it difficult to believe in the **Resurrection** until the *"last day."* (John 11: 24) She had doubts about His resurrection even in face of the fact that Jesus had just told her that her brother would rise again. (Verse 23) On that occasion Jesus declared to her that He was the **resurrection** and the **life** and that those who would believe on Him, even though they were **dead**, yet they would **live**. (John 11: 25)

Mary of Magdala

While all of the Gospel writers give an account of Jesus' resurrection, and there is no contradiction in any of them, there are facts that individual writers give that others do not give. John gives us a poignant account of Mary Magdalene and her activity on the day of Jesus' resurrection. She went early to the tomb. The word John uses for "early" is **proi** (πρωι). It refers to a time when the world is beginning to awaken. It is not night anymore but it is not yet day. Mary could not go on the day before because it was the Sabbath and it would have been unlawful but now it is dawning toward the first day of the week and she was anxious to

25

visit the tomb of her Lord. Therefore, at the earliest lawful moment she was to be found at the tomb.

When Mary arrived at the tomb, she saw the stone taken away. The word used to describe her seeing of the stone was "**blepo**" (βλεπω). That means that she glanced at the empty tomb but had no understanding of what had really happened. She returned quickly to tell Peter and John about it. Her word to them was, *"They have taken away the Lord out of the tomb and **we do not know where they have laid Him.**"* She has not yet understood that He has been resurrected from the dead.

Peter and John ran immediately to the tomb. John ran ahead of Peter and simply glanced into the tomb. When John, arriving before Peter, glanced into the tomb, the same word that we have mentioned is used ("*blepo*"). When Peter arrived, he went into the tomb. The word used for Peter is "**theoreo**" (θεωρεω). It indicates a careful perusal of the details in the situation. While the word used to describe John's first sight of the clothes was also "**blepo**" as was used concerning Mary but in verse 6, there is a closer examination concerning the significance of what has happened. The word used to describe John's second viewing is **eidon** (ειδον). This word indicates seeing with **understanding**. Finally, John understands what it is all about. He sees the linen cloths laying there folded and undisturbed. If there had been grave robbers, the grave clothes would not have been there. It is clear that Jesus had simply disappeared from the grave clothes and left them intact. The angels did not roll the stone away in order to let Jesus **out**. They rolled the stone away to let the disciples **in**. Now, John, that disciple whom Jesus loved, has **seen** or understood and he has **believed.** (John 20: 8) John makes it clear that until this time they had not understood the Scriptures that He must rise again from the dead (John 20: 9).

Matthew records that there was a shaking of the earth when the angel of the Lord descended from Heaven and rolled back the stone. The earth shook when He **died** at Calvary and the earth shook when He **arose** from the grave. It is as though the greatest event in all of human history is transpiring. Jesus is the first fruits of them that slept. (I Corinthians 15: 30) No one has ever been resurrected before. Some have been resuscitated but Jesus came forth out of the grave with a different glorified body.

His Body

Mary did not expect to see Jesus alive. As previously mentioned, when she had rushed back to Peter and John her exclamation was, "*They have taken away the Lord out of the tomb, and we do not know **where they have laid Him**.*" As far as she was concerned, He was still dead. As stated above, it was John who first realized the full significance of what he was seeing. Peter and John had returned to the other disciples but Mary lingered near the tomb. When she finally recognized Jesus, He said to her: "*Do not cling to me for I have not yet ascended to My Father, but go and tell My brethren and say to them, I am ascending to My Father and your Father and to My God and your God.*" (John 20: 17) What was Jesus really saying to Mary? It was not that He did not want her to touch Him for He later invited the disciples to touch His resurrection body. Mary was confused when she saw Him alive she thought that His life of teaching and fellowship would continue as it was before and Jesus was announcing to her that things would be different because He would ascend to the Father. That was the message that she was to bear to their circle of friends.

Thomas

Belief did not come easy to Thomas. On the evening of Resurrection day when Jesus appeared in the midst of the

27

disciples, He breathed upon them and said, "*Receive the Holy Spirit.*" It is the same root word (emphusao – εμφυσαο) used in the Septuagint to translate Genesis 2: 7 and Ezekiel 37: 9. The Septuagint is the translation of the Old Testament into Greek. The New Testament, of course, was written in Greek. Just as man, in the beginning, received life through the breath of God, so the power of the Spirit was imparted to the disciples by the breath of Jesus, the God/Man. It was a foretaste of the wonderful things that would happen to the disciples on the day of Pentecost. Thomas was not there on that occasion and when the other disciples told Thomas that they had seen the Lord, Thomas could not believe. It was not as though he did not love Christ. He was simply honest enough to confess that he could not believe until he saw evidence. He said, "*Unless I see in His hands the print of the nails, and put my finger into the print of the nails, and put my hand into His side, I will not believe.*" (John 20: 25) Yes, Thomas was having a struggle. He was always a man who wanted to see evidence. He wanted proof. (see John 14: 5) It was eight days later, however, that His disciples were again shut up in the room and Thomas was with them. Jesus appeared in their midst. Then He addressed Thomas. He was kind to him. He called upon Thomas to "*reach your finger here and look at my hands; and reach your hand here, and put it into my side. Do not be unbelieving, but believing.*" Then, Thomas answered Him, "*My Lord and My God.*" Jesus' response to Thomas was one that all Christians should forever remember when He said, "Thomas, because you have seen me, you have believed. Blessed are those who have not seen and yet have believed." (see John 20: 26-29) The command of Jesus to His disciples that they should spread the good news was a recurring one. On the occasion when He breathed upon them the power of the Holy Spirit, He had said, "As the Father has sent me, I also send you." What a Savior!

His Glorified Body

We do not understand some things about Jesus' resurrection body. On the evening of resurrection day, the disciples were in a room with the doors shut. The text indicates that the door was fastened. Suddenly, Jesus appeared in their midst and said, *"Peace be with you."*

We do not understand everything about the body of Jesus after His resurrection. The New Testament writers do not try to hide the fear and the doubt that His disciples had when they saw His **resurrection body**. There was a reason why Jesus said, *"Peace be unto you."* Luke points out that they were terrified and thought that they had seen a ghost. To that, Jesus responded by saying, *"Behold My hands and My feet, that it is I Myself: handle me, and see; for spirit hath not flesh and bones as you see Me have"*. On that occasion, they gave Him a piece of broiled fish and a honeycomb and He did eat before them. He then explained to them that *"these are the words which I spake unto you while I was with you, that all things must be fulfilled, which were written in the Law of Moses, and the prophets, and in the Psalms concerning Me."* (Luke 24: 39 - 44) At that point, Jesus began to open their understanding that they might understand the **Scriptures. That is the most important understanding any man can gain.** He then said, *"Thus it is written, and thus it behooved Christ to suffer, and to **rise from the dead the third day**: and that **repentance and remission of sins** should be **preached in His name** among all nations beginning at Jerusalem."* (Verse 45-47 KJV)

Jesus declared to them *"... a spirit hath not flesh and bones, as you see me have ...."*. We know, therefore, that Jesus' resurrection body had flesh and bone and that it was not simply a spiritual body but a glorified body. John never laid claim to a complete understanding. In his first epistle he said, *"Beloved, now are we children of God; and it has not yet been revealed what we shall be,*

29

*but **we know that when He is revealed, we shall be like Him,** for we shall see Him as He is."* (I John 3: 2) It was enough for John that we would have a body like that of Jesus. He appeared through closed doors. He could transport Himself over great distances in a short time. He could eat food. He had recognizable qualities about Him. John is saying that we can be sure that our bodies will contain all the characteristics of Jesus' glorified body when He returns to earth to receive us unto Himself and that was enough for John.

More Evidence

There is **more evidence** that Jesus lived, died, and rose from the grave than there is to support the existence of any other world figure from George Washington, to King James, to Charlemagne, to Tiberius Caesar, to Socrates or Aristotle. When an attorney pleads his case, he feels that he has established the facts when he has the testimony of two or three witnesses. Jesus made ten appearances to His disciples after His resurrection. The Apostle Paul points out that there was a meeting in which more than **five hundred people saw Jesus at one time** (I Corinthians 15: 6). His final appearance to a man on earth was to the Apostle Paul on the Damascus Road (Acts 9: 3-8). We submit that there is no other figure in all of human history whose reality is so firmly established as that of **Jesus Christ our Lord**.

Josephus

This fact of history was so well established that even the famed Jewish historian called Flavius Josephus wrote about it. He said:

"Now there was about this time Jesus, a wise man, if it be lawful to call Him a man for He was a doer of wonderful works - a teacher of such men as received the truth with pleasure. He drew over to Him both many of the Jews, and many of the Gentiles. He was the Christ; and when Pilate, at the suggestion of the principal men amongst us, had condemned Him to the cross, those who loved Him at the first did not forsake Him, for He appeared to them alive again **the third day** as the divine prophets had foretold these and ten thousand other wonderful things concerning Him; and the tribe of Christians, so named from Him, are not extinct at this day." (Josephus, Antiq. 18. 3. 1. ff)

This is not to suggest that Christians should heavily rely upon Josephus because he is not always an un-impeccable source. This is simply to point out how widely known the Resurrection of Jesus was. We began this chapter with the question as to whether or not we can believe that Jesus is and was real. The answer is **absolutely** and **unshakably: "Yes."**

John's final word on the situation was, *"This is the disciple who testifies of these things and wrote these things and we know that his testimony is true."* (John 21: 24) The word that is translated "testimony" is **marturia** (μαρτυρια). In the gospel of John, it is translated four times as testimony. It is also translated as "witness." We get our word martyr from this word. It means to **bear testimony unto death or by death**. The same word is used in Acts 1: 8 where Jesus said, " ... You shall receive power when the Holy Spirit is come upon you; and you shall be witnesses to me in Jerusalem, and in Judea and Samaria, and unto the end of the earth." That is exactly what happened to most of those disciples standing there. They bore witness to Christ either by their death or until death!

Conclusion

As we have seen, Jesus performed miracles in order to authenticate His mission on earth. As far as scholars can determine, He performed over 350 miracles. The miracles provided proof that He was the **Messiah** and the **Son of God.** Jesus repeatedly stated that He performed the miracles or the great works in order that men might **believe.** He pointed out in John 5 that *"The Father loveth the Son and **showeth** Him all things that He Himself doeth: and He will show Him greater works than these that ye may marvel."* (KJV) The central theme of His ministry was that He was the Son of God and that He had come into the world to **redeem man from sin.** He continued this theme as He was on the way to the tomb of Lazarus whom He would raise from the dead. When He announced to the Disciples that their friend Lazarus was dead, he forthrightly spoke unto them and said, *"I am glad for your sakes that I was not there, **to the intent ye may believe...**"* (John 11: 15 KJV) When Jesus was pointing out to His Disciples that He was the only way to the Father and access to the Father was through Him alone, He reminded them of the mighty works that He had done and that He was able to perform the mighty works (miracles) because and He and the Father were **one** and that the **Father dwelt in Him.** His plea to them was, *"Believe Me that I am in the Father, and the Father is in Me: or else **believe Me for the very works sake.**"* This theme continued throughout the ministry of Jesus and He made it perfectly evident that our salvation depended upon our believing in Him as the Son of God: that He was in the Father and that the Father dwelt in Him. There is to be **no substitute for Jesus Christ.** There is no other way of salvation. No matter how serious one may be in embracing some other kind of religion, it is only through Jesus Christ that we may have salvation. It is a **mockery** to say that we can have salvation **in any other way** when God sent His only Son into the world who would pay the penalty for our sins on the cross at Calvary and ascended unto the Father 40 days later. If there was ever any other way of salvation we would never have heard of the crown of thorns, the mocking by Roman soldiers, the thud of the hammer as they drove nails into His hands and feet or that moment when Jesus bore our Hell as He cried out from Calvary's cross, *"My God, My God, why hast Thou forsaken Me!" Just before* "He yielded up the ghost," He said, "It is finished." That settled it all. The task of redemption was complete and there was no other way of redemption. No matter what kind of religion man may concoct; no matter how ceremonious and beautiful it may seem, no matter how devoted its' followers, there is no other way than that of Jesus and Him crucified!

Chapter Two
Can We Believe In Divine Creation?

One of the most pungent and biting questions on the scene today is, "Can we believe in the divine creation of the universe?" Man has more Biblical and scientific evidence today in support of divine creation than we have ever known before. That is the reason it is so important for the reader to read this **entire chapter**. Again, we go to the great Apostle John. This man, who walked so closely with Jesus while He was on earth, confirms the Genesis account of creation in the first verse of his gospel. After John identifies Jesus as the "Word", he reiterates that Jesus was with God **in the beginning**. It is in verse 3 that John declares Jesus to have been active with **God in creation**. He makes it clear that there was not one single thing that was created without Jesus. In this passage, John confirms the creation account in Genesis 1, which states clearly that it was "**in the beginning**" that **God created the heavens and the earth**. There have been numerous accommodation theories about creation most of which turn out to be utter nonsense. Some try to translate the Hebrew word "*hayethah*" as "became" instead of "was" and that in verse 3 Moses begins to record the **re-creation** of the universe. The accommodationists try to squeeze in millions of years between verses 2 and 3. There is absolutely no reason to do this and there is no support in the rest of Scripture to support such an irrational idea.

Others have embraced the so-called "day-age" theory. This theory contends that the various days listed in the account of creation represent geological ages. Again, there is **absolutely no**

scientific or scriptural evidence to support such an idea. It was simply an attempt to work out some kind of syllogism between biblical scholars and the Darwinists. Again, there is absolutely no reason for it and as most accommodation theories go, it tends to **diminish** the **authority of Scripture** and make biblical believers the laughing stock of the world. Let us make clear, at this point, that the most reliable source of authority in the world is **Biblical Scripture**. The more we learn about Scripture through archaeological discoveries and historical findings, the more reverence we have for the **Word of God**.

Not only does John confirm the Genesis account of creation in the first chapter of his gospel but he reiterates it in his first epistle. In the epistle of I John, he testifies of seeing, hearing and touching Jesus. Jesus was no apparition and he states clearly that Jesus was *"from the beginning."* (I John 1:1) He also identifies Jesus as the *"word of life."* He also states in verse 2 that Jesus was **with the Father** and was **manifested** unto us. He declares these truths in his epistles in order that we can have fellowship with the saints and our fellowship is altogether with the **Father and His Son, Jesus Christ**. John states clearly that he is writing these things so that *"our joy might be full."* (Verse 4)

Moreover, Jesus Himself confirms His presence with the Father *"before the world was."* (John 17: 5) Jesus also made it clear that the Father had loved Him before the **foundation of the world** (John 17:24).

Jesus again confirmed divine creation when some Pharisees asked Him a question about divorce. Jesus' answer to them was, *"Have you not read, that **He** which **made them in the beginning** made them **male and female**."* (Matthew 19: 4) There is no indication that man and woman were self generated out of some primeval scum or that they came from some lower life form but they were created by a living God. So, the question is, who will we believe? Will we believe **Jesus**, the **Son** of **God**, and the Savior of the world or will we believe some anti-God fanatic who wishes to discredit the Word of almighty God? That is the decision that every Christian must make!

Other Evidence

There is other compelling evidence of fiat creation by a living God. The Psalmist declared that the world is full of the goodness of God. He stated his case in Psalm 33: 6 when he said, *"By the word of the Lord were the heavens made; and all the hosts of them by the breath of His mouth."* The Psalmist further said *"... He spake and it was done; He commandeth and it stood fast."* (Verse 9) It is in the book of Hebrews that we have another affirmation of the creative acts of God who *"hath in these days spoken unto us by His Son whom He hath appointed heir of all things, **by whom also He made the worlds ...**"* (Hebrews 1: 1-2) He presses the case further when he said: *"... thou, Lord, **in the beginning** hast laid the foundation of the earth; and the heavens are the works of thy hands."* (Verse 10) At this point, the writer of Hebrews was quoting from Psalm 103: 25. Therefore, we have another double affirmation of the creative acts of God. It is a reiteration of Psalm 96: 5 which says, *"... the **Lord made** the heavens."*

Paul's Teaching

The Apostle Paul undergirds it when he said, "God, who commanded the light to shine out of darkness, hath shined in our hearts to give the light of the knowledge of the glory of God in the face of Jesus Christ." (II Corinthians 4: 6) The writer of Hebrews presses the same thing when he says that the worlds were framed "by the **word of God**, so that things which are seen were not made of things which do appear." That means that God **spoke** the world into existence ex-nihilo (out of nothing). That is the mighty power

37

of a creating God and it comes from the most reliable source on the face of the earth - the Scriptures of the Old and New Testaments. (Hebrews 11: 3) On the fifth day of creation, God brought forth sea life and fowls that fly in the open firmament of heaven. On the sixth day, God brought forth land animals and other creeping things as well as the beasts of the earth. All these would reproduce "after His kind." There is nothing, whatever, to indicate self-generation of any kind of life on the planet. Everything was created by a living God. All of these activities are recorded in the first chapter of Genesis and confirmed by many other Scriptures.

From Whence Comes the Problem?

In the Nineteenth Century, three things happened that have profoundly affected Christianity and left many Christians in a state of confusion. We will examine them briefly to help the reader understand what is behind some of the things that we are hearing today.

First: Karl Marx, in 1848, was expelled from Germany and found a haven of refuge in London and a supporter in Friedrich Engles. He had been trained in the philosophy of Immanuel Kant, George Hegel, and Ludwig Feuerbach. Feuerback stated that he was an "anti-theist." Marx was born in the Rhineland of Jewish parents who became Lutherans. They were, apparently, nominal Lutherans who were not serious about their faith. Marx finally rejected Hegel and Feuerbach and embraced the Communist idea that reality is found only in matter and how man responds to matter. It would later be called "dialectical materialism" since all meaning would be related to matter. He spent much of his time in London agitating and gathering evidence from the British Museum for his indictment of capitalism in his work that would be published called "Das Kapital" (1867). Marx was an atheist and he, along with Engles, published **"The Communist Manifesto"** (1848). Marx felt that history was moving inexorably toward a communist society. He believed that a communist society would be firmly established, private property would be a thing of the past, and the state itself would **manage everything**. Of course, those societies that have tried Communism have found that it has never delivered on that promise. Thus, Karl Marx (1818 - 1883) became the Father of what we know as Communism. While Marx was an Atheist, there were still some things that bothered him. He and Engles called upon the so-called "down trodden proletariat" to unite and overthrow the capitalistic orders in order to usher in a new society. The movement swept across Europe and finally came to America. Many of the self-styled "intellectuals" on American university campuses embraced Marxism. The American Communist Party grew to be a sizable and threatening organization during the 30's and 40's. It probably reached its' zenith during and immediately after World War II. Many Marxists made their way into the Roosevelt Administration and many were held over in the Truman Administration. It is not known whether Presidents Roosevelt or Truman knew who the Soviet spies were in their administrations. Stalin had been an ally during World War II and President Roosevelt referred to him as "Uncle Joe." President Truman said of Stalin, "I like old Joe. Joe is a decent fellow."

Venona Project

Stalin and his henchmen thought they had an unbreakable code but some intelligence men in the US Army broke the code. The operation was called the Venona Project. On July 11, 1995, the US Government released a cache of Soviet cables that had been decoded during the Cold War. It was a very secret undertaking. The cables revealed that Julius and Ethel Rosenberg were, indeed,

Soviet spies and they had delivered atomic secrets to the Soviet Union. They were very close assistants to the President. Alger Hiss, who had gone with Roosevelt to Yalta and had urged him to give control of Eastern Europe to Stalin, after the war, was also tried and sent to prison for espionage. Henry Wallace, Vice-president from 1940 - 1944, ran against Truman in 1948 on the "Progressive Party" ticket with the support of the American Communist Party and the party's paper known as the Daily Worker. Some leaders of the President's Party had told him that Wallace could not be on the ticket in 1944 and President Roosevelt was angered with them about it. They gave him Harry Truman whom he obviously disliked and he did not share critical information about what was going on concerning the Manhattan Project or the progress of World War II. Wherever Wallace campaigned, he drew large crowds but he did not glean many votes in the election. If Wallace had been on the Vice-Presidential ticket in 1944, he would have become President when Roosevelt passed away. That would have been disastrous. Leaders of the party knew that Roosevelt was sick and were fearful that he would not be able to serve the full term. They also knew that Henry Wallace would never do in the Office of President. When the Soviet cables were de-classified, it was worse than anyone thought. America had almost fallen under the grip of Communism. It was difficult for Americans to imagine. The Rosenbergs were tried and executed for their dastardly acts of delivering atomic secrets to the Soviet Union. Some of the Communists in the administration fled the country and became advisors to Communist regimes in other parts of the world.

Turning Point

During the 50's, when Americans saw the **ruthlessness** and the **millions** killed by the Stalin regime, members walked away from the American Communist Party and the membership in the Party dramatically diminished but, make no mistake about it, many are still around and their goals are still the same. When a people believe that there is no **sovereign God;** then they believe that man is master of his own destiny and there are always those around who are just sure that **they** know what is best for everyone else! They persuade themselves that they are more intelligent than anyone else and they feel that they have to control the lives of others. Such people are always **dangerous!** Marxism is in a **resurgent** mode today and Americans will be **wise** to keep a wary eye on them.

Second: The second thing that happened in the nineteenth century came in 1859. Charles Darwin published his major work on Evolution and Carl Marx loved it because, in his sick mind, it enabled him to explain the origin of man without God. The work was called "The Origin of Species." However, Darwin was not the first to advocate Evolution. It had its advocates all the way from the Greek philosopher Anaximander, right on up to Darwin's Grandfather, Erasmus Darwin. His Grandfather was a physician. It was said that his Grandfather liked cream on his food. In those days, he probably didn't realize what it was doing to him but he had gotten so big that he had to have a special table built for his dining room with a half moon cutout so that he could fit his "tummy" into it and get up to the table to eat. He was not only a physician but he was something of a backyard botanist. Charles Darwin studied medicine at Edinburgh for a while but did not do well there. He then decided that it would be nice to be the pastor of a country parish, so he began studying theology at Cambridge without much success. Then he gave up his dream of becoming a country clergyman. Darwin had spent the summer of 1825 as an apprentice doctor with his father, helping him to treat the poor of Shropshire. He and his brother had entered medical school at Edinburgh in the Fall of 1825. He found surgery distressing and neglected his studies. He then learned taxidermy from John Edmond Stone, a free black man who had accompanied Charles Waterton into the South American Rain Forest.

Second Year

In his second year he had joined the Plinian Society; supposedly, a group of students interested in natural history but their debates often strayed into radical materialism. He had assisted Robert Edmond Grant's research into the anatomy and life cycle of marine invertebrates. While at Cambridge, he read Pali's **"Natural Theology"** which argued for Divine design in nature and describing adaptation as God's acting through nature. He also made a close friend of John Steven Henslow. It was Henslow's influence and arrangements that got Charles Darwin the assignment to travel on the HMS Beagle with Captain Robert Fitzroy. It was an oceanic survey of the coastline of Western South America. Darwin's father financed the trip. He rejected the trip at first as a waste of time but he was finally persuaded to finance the trip by his brother-in-law Josiah Wedgewood. While the voyage lasted for almost five years, Darwin did not, as some have thought, spend that much time on the Galapagos Islands (located in a small archipelago off the northwest coast of South America). The HMS Beagle returned and docked at Falmouth, Cornwall on October 2, 1836. After visiting his family, he made his way back to Cambridge and to his friend, Henslow, who helped him organize for the encoding of life specimens by class, phylum, and order. In October, he met Charles Lyle who introduced him to other naturalists and assisted him in finding lodging at Cambridge. In early March, he moved to London and there became a part of Lyle's social circle where he met such influential people as Charles Babbage. It was there that Darwin began to discuss **transmutations**. Henslow assisted him in obtaining a treasury grant of a **thousand pounds**, which would amount to about **seventy-five thousand pounds** in today's currency.

Health Problems

While Darwin was on the Beagle, he was plagued with seasickness. After accepting the duties as Secretary of the Geological Society, the strain of the work took a toll on his health. He suffered episodes of stomach pains, vomiting, severe boils, palpitations, trembling, and other symptoms, particularly during times of stress. Poor health plagued him the rest of his life. On January 29, 1839, Darwin married his cousin, Emma Wedgewood, at Maer in an Anglican ceremony. His wife, a Unitarian, expressed her concern that because of their different beliefs, they would not be together in the after-life. Finally, Darwin and his friends discovered that **Alfred Russell Wallace** was working on his volume called "Introduction of Species" that covered much of the **same ground** as Darwin's work would cover. Darwin rushed into publication and struggled for 13 months to produce an abstract of his "**big book**." While he was suffering from ill health, he got constant encouragement from his friend, Charles Lyell. It was Lyell who arranged to have the book rushed into publication by John Murray. On November 22, 1859, the book went to the booksellers. An initial run of 1,250 copies were sold almost immediately.

The Darwins' had 10 children, two of whom died in infancy, and his daughter, Annie, died at the age of 10. He often wondered aloud if his children had inherited weaknesses because he had married his cousin.

Darwin remained close friends with his vicar at Downe, John Innes, and continued for a while to play a part in the work of the parish. It was around 1849 that he ceased to be active in the church and would go for a walk on Sundays while his family attended church. His reason was that he considered it "**absurd** to think that a man might be an ardent **Theist** and an **evolutionist**." In his last years, he stated that he had "never been an atheist in the sense of denying the existence of God." However, he said, "I think that generally ... an agnostic would be the most correct description of my state of mind." The word "agnostic" had been coined by Darwin supporter, Thomas Huxley. There was a "Lady Hope" story published in 1915 claiming that Charles Darwin had reverted to his Christian faith on his deathbed. That claim, however, was repudiated by Darwin's children.

Inhumane Eugenics

Some of the most vicious and inhumane things imaginable have been foisted upon humankind because of the evolutionary hypothesis. One of the most barbaric, fiendish and neronian practices that came out of Darwinism was eugenics. It was a forced sterilization of people who were considered too genetically inferior to reproduce. Despots all over the civilized world latched on to Darwinism, which later became known as "Social Darwinism." It flourished in America as well as in Europe and Asia, especially in the early Twentieth Century. In the United States, there were physicians, psychologists, and white Protestants of Northern European ancestry who embraced eugenics. On **Long Island,** there was a genetics research center at a place called **Cold Spring Harbor where eugenics was forced upon innocent people..** The Director was Charles B. Davenport who was a zoologist and in **full support of Darwinism**. The theory of Gregory Mendel was resurrected around 1900. He believed that genetics controlled a number of diseases and mental deficiencies that were classified as "**feeble mindedness**". These people decided that such maladies as criminality, poverty, alcoholism, and prostitution sprang from mental deficiencies, especially among **immigrants from Southern Europe**. These people thought they had "**scientific proof**" concerning their conclusions and they joined others who wanted to **restrict immigration** from Southern Europe. Many of them advocated sterilization of certain groups, arguing that it would reduce the spread of **bad genes** among lower income groups. Many contended that mentally deficient people were reproducing at a rate high enough to constitute a menace and advocated **forced sterilization** for those they deemed to be "**feeble minded**". In most cases, it was nothing more than deafness caused by such things as measles.

Immigration Restricted

This group supported the passage of the Immigration Restriction Act of 1924. They gave **biological reason**s for the severe reductions it imposed on immigration of people from Eastern and Southern Europe. Finally, **two dozen states enacted eugenic sterilization laws**. The US Supreme Court even upheld the constitutionality of such measures in the case of Buck vs. Bell (1927). It was Justice **Oliver Wendell Holmes Jr.**, the darling **her**o of the **left wing radicals**, who wrote the **majority opinion**. He stated, "three generations of imbeciles are enough." By the mid-1930s, forced sterilizations had been performed on about 20,000 people in the United States. According to Daniel J. Kevles, some of the leading states in enforcing the act were California and Virginia. However, some states gave little attention to the enforcement of the act. Of course, the practice finally took on a **racial** component. Finally, geneticists learned that diseases and physical traits were not the result of single genes and that human behavior is the product of a complex interplay between **biology** and **environment**. They learned that the target population might have differed in **ethnic** and **cultural** factors rather than the biological area . They also learned, as mentioned earlier, that **many** of those whom they thought to be "feeble minded" simply had **hearing problems**, sometimes associated with Rubella, and were as **intelligent** as anyone else. Many, however, felt that they must acquiesce to the "**sacred cow**" of "**science**." It has recently been discovered that much of that "science" was **junk science.** Some of the victims and their families have sued a number of those states that participated in the barbaric sterilization policy. At this writing, the state of North Carolina is trying to settle claims with the families of eugenics victims.

Of course, **Adolph Hitler** was a great **believer** in **Darwinian evolution**, which inspired him in his diabolical plan to create a "**super race**." He actually developed a breeding program in which young healthy girls were placed in a camp and his "choice" men from among the SS and Gestapo groups were sent to "breed" them. Numerous people in Europe and especially Norway today are hated because they were babies who were born of that "super race" experiment of Hitler.

Evolution's Holocaust

However, Hitler was no worse than Stalin, Mussolini, or Mao. These men with their laws and armies put over 100,000,000 people to death by armed suppression or deliberate starvation. Again, we see that when there is no belief in God there is no moral compass for the people or their leaders. When we view man as nothing more than a higher form of animal life, as evolution does, **who is surprised if he acts like an animal**! With the rise of evolutionary teachings in the public schools and universities of America has come insidious, malevolent behavior and ruthless, savage crimes. What happens in a nation when children are taught that we have evolved from some lower animal life and that we or the world in which we live was not created by God? The result is that there is no sense of accountability to a living God and they start acting like the animals that they have been taught that they came from. For instance, on March 29, 2010, Phoebe Prince of South Hadley, Massachusetts committed suicide after intensive bullying by other students both at school and on the Internet. Her parents had brought her here from Ireland because they wanted her to **experience America**! At the time of the news announcement, nine students have been charged, some for statutory rape. She attended the South Hadley High School. That is not the only case of tragedy. There have been shootings in other schools. A young twelve-year-old boy recently shot his Father's pregnant fiancée and killed her. Another North Carolina mother killed five children including her own and then killed herself.

There are unbelievable stories about mothers killing their children and parents killing one another. Many of the babies born in America these days are born out of wedlock. Single parents are causing a terrible drain on the national economy. Prisons are overflowing. Children are being abandoned. That is what happens in a society when its' children are taught the evolutionary myth that they evolved from lower animal life and that they were not created by a living God. If there is no responsibility to a living God then there is chaos. Sexual perverts and predators are demanding special treatment. We have to ask, "Has the evolutionary hypothesis brought any good to mankind?" The answer is a resounding **No**! It is not only a lie but it is also **harmful**!

Aggressive Evolutionists

When Evolutionists in America began to encounter Christian resistance, they became very vicious and they developed a new paradigm. Christians had to be smeared and they must be made an example to anyone who would dare to challenge the **evolutionary nonsense**. The backers of evolution had to be portrayed as intellectuals, professionals, or scientists. Christians who opposed the evolutionary theory were to be portrayed as "flat earth" people who were ignorant and worshipped by handling snakes. This paradigm was never more on display than at Dayton, Tennessee during the **Scopes Trial** in which a biology teacher had violated Tennessee law by teaching the evolutionary hypothesis as scientific truth. The hypothesis was not considered science and the state of Tennessee ruled that, since it was not science, it was not to be taught in a science classroom. One would **think by the news reports** coming out of Dayton that Clarence Darrow actually **won the case**. He did not. William Jennings Bryan had assisted the prosecution and **the prosecution won the case**. John Scopes was convicted and fined. The case generated widespread interest and the town was turned into a circus scene, largely by the Press.

Biased Press

It will not surprise Americans to know that the Press was biased, even in those days. It was during the zenith of the so-called "Progressive" movement. Of course, wherever there are large gatherings of people there will be hawkers. Some were selling souvenirs, including "sock monkeys." There have been some reports that a religious cult of snake handlers came out of the mountains for the trial although that was never confirmed. William Jennings Bryan was known as the "orator with the golden throat." Near the end of the trial, he allowed himself to be "suckered" into a situation in which he could be put on the witness stand where he was not allowed to respond after the questioning by Darrow. Clarence Darrow was reported to be a "brilliant" lawyer but he was more shrewd than smart. Bryan was a diabetic at a time when treatment of diabetes was very inadequate. He died 5 days after the trial from diabetes-induced exhaustion, not because he was so overwhelmed by the trial. The **reporting** of the Scopes Trial, often identified as the "monkey trial," was very one sided and biased in favor of the **evolutionary nonsense**. This was the kind of paradigm that existed for many years and still exists today. It was the same kind of atmosphere that swept Woodrow Wilson into office a few years earlier who turned out to be the most inept and leftwing President in modern times. It was during the so-called "gilded age." Americans knew that they were in an unprecedented era of prosperity brought about by the industrial revolution.

Marxist Confusion

People like the **Marxist,** Leon Trotsky, who lived in New York, could not understand it. Trotsky was able to rent an apartment in New York for $18.00 a month with full conveniences such as electricity, gas, bathroom, telephone service, an automatic service elevator, and a chute for his garbage. He could not believe that capitalism could bring about such prosperity for ordinary working people. He had just been **sure** that Americans would **embrace Communism** but they did not. The German socialist, **August Bebel** predicted in 1907 that Americans would be the first to usher in a socialist republic **but they refused it**. Inventions were blossoming. Patents were being issued daily. In 1892, the United States reached a favorable balance of trade.

The American people knew that the growth and prosperity was the result of 30 years of growth from the most powerful economic engine ever known but the left wing progressives thought that America was ripe for a socialist-communist takeover. Schweikart and Allen said it well in their 829 page **History of the United States** when they pointed out:

" 'Professionalism' and 'Scientific' became the buzz word of the day. To many, science had become the new God and the

49

theories of Darwin, Freud, and Marx convinced people that only those things one could prove through experimentation were valid - despite the fact that Darwin, Marx, or Freud had never proven anything scientifically." (Page 459)

Is It Scientific?

The word science comes from a Latin word **scientia**, which means, "to know" or "have knowledge of." The **scientific method** refers to the "principle of collecting data through observation as well as experimentation, formulation and testing of hypotheses." That is the way Webster describes it. Obviously, **evolution is not scientific**. It is apparent that the idea of evolution being "scientific" is a deceitful aberration. All the claims that evolution is scientific show it to be the **delusional and fictitious nonsense** that it is. Nothing can be called scientific unless it can be **observed** and evolution **has never been observed**. It has been built upon a series of hoaxes. From the so-called "Piltdown Man" to the alleged "Nebraska Man" the hypothetical evolution of man has been a sham. The "Piltdown Man" was found to be the skeletal remains of an Orangutan that were found many yards apart. The "Nebraska Man" was built around one tooth. After much research and the finding of other similar teeth, it was learned that the tooth, around which Harold Cooke had built the "Nebraska Man," was the tooth of a pig that is now extinct on the North American Continent. Always, the evolutionists are contending that the "missing link" is just around the corner, all the way from "Lucy" to the "Ice Man." When responsible anthropologists have examined the evidence, it has been found to be utterly false.

About The Horse

This writer once visited the display supposedly showing the evolution of the horse that was being carried on a tour among college campuses in this country. Having been reared as a child around horses, I had some familiarity with them. When I viewed the so-called "evolution of the horse," I noted that there was the skeleton of a miniature horse. The skeletal remains were real. There was also the skeleton of a pony (probably a Shetland pony). I rode one when I was a child. Then, there were the remains of a large horse. The other so-called "skeletons" were all made from plaster of paris. What are the facts? Miniature horses are still being bred. In fact, this writer lives near a horse farm where some miniature horses are bred. In western North Carolina, a breeder breeds very small miniature horses that are purchased for pets. Miniature horses range all the way from 18 inches high to 30 inches. There is nothing new about miniature horses and they represent **nothing** in the so-called "**evolutionary chain**." The entire display was phony as far as proving anything about evolution but as I viewed it, I observed gullible college students who knew nothing about horses but they were overawed and almost "giddy" about seeing the **so-called evolution of the horse!**

In order for anything to be considered scientific there must be the ability to observe and either verify or falsify. If that cannot be done, then it is not scientific. With evolution, there is no way to observe it taking place nor can it be verified or falsified. To claim that it is "science" is to do violence to the term. It is nothing more than amphigoric blather. Thus, we clearly understand that evolution is **not science. It is an anti-God philosophy that serves as under-penning for activist atheists.**

51

With known information today, it serves no scientific purpose and explains nothing. Its' only possible purpose in this day is to prop up the senseless philosophy of atheism. One of the most widely known atheists of today is Stephen Hawking. He is one of the world's most famous living scientists. For many years, he held the prestigious Lucasian professorship at Cambridge University, a position once held by Sir Isaac Newton. He holds numerous doctoral degrees and is a Companion of Honour at the Court of the Queen of England. He has suffered the ravages of motor neuron disease for over 40 years. He has been confined to a wheel chair for a long time and speaks only with a voice synthesizer. This well-known physicist contends that philosophy is dead and that there is no God. His claim is disputed by none other than John C. Lennox, MA, PhD, DPhil, and DSc, who is a professor at the University of Oxford and fellow in Mathematics and the Philosophy of Science at Green Templeton College. He has very successfully debated such atheists as Richard Dawkins and Christopher Hitchings. Hitchings recently passed away at the age of 57 with cancer of the esophagus. He was associated with the New York Times. Hawking is famous for his studies of black holes. His work has led to the prediction of "Hawking Radiation." If this discovery is verified experimentally, many feel that he should be a recipient of the Nobel Peace Prize. Hawking contends that the universe is self-created through the laws of nature.

Paley's View

The great philosopher William Paley contends that a law of nature, in and of itself, presupposes an agent because it is only the mode through which the agent proceeds and requires a power behind it. Without an empowering agent, the law can do nothing and is nothing. Standing alone, such laws cannot even cause anything let alone create it. Dr. John Lennox bears this out when he says, "The laws of physics are not only incapable of creating anything; they cannot even cause anything to happen. For instance, Newton's celebrated laws of motion never caused a pool ball to race across the green felt table. People using a pool cue and the action of their own muscles can only do that. The laws enable us to analyze the motion, and to map the trajectory of the ball's movement in the future (providing nothing external interferes); but they are powerless to move the ball let alone bring it into existence." Therefore, Dr. Hawking's idea of a self-generated universe is totally without foundation and is unbelievably primitive and shallow in its concept, revealing the presence of pandemonial thought patterns. Dr. John Lennox further points out that, "The God in whom Galileo, Kepler, Descartes, and Newton believed was not merely the embodiment of the laws of nature. He was (and is) the intelligent creator and upholder of the universe, who is a person and not a set of abstract laws. He was, in fact, the God of the Bible. Such pioneer scientists as those mentioned here believed in a living God who created all things made. Therefore, there was Divine order in the universe that man could learn about."

It is the claim of Hawking and many other atheists that those who believe in the living God simply use the laws of nature to define God. That is far from truth. God is defined by the living Word of God that presents God as the living God whom we can know and have fellowship with and who is the creator of all things (John 1: 1-5). Many of the atheists step perilously close to embracing the pagan gods of nature, which is the very thing that happened to the Apostle Paul at Lystra. When he rejected their pagan theology of many gods, they stoned him and left him for dead. Paul had pointed out that it is the living God who gives us rain upon the earth and the seasons to produce good things for us and not pagan gods. Sir Isaac Newton so believed in perfect order in the universe that his discovery of the laws of motion enabled scientists to develop the calculations that placed a man on the moon and it was Einstein's Theory of Relativity that gave us a peek into the velocity of light that led to the development of atomic energy. All of these things came about because our world was created by an intelligent being who is also behind all the laws of physics and nature.

We live in an information age. When we see a few letters of the alphabet spelling our name in the sand, as Dr. Lennox points out, we immediately recognize it as the work of an intelligent agent. How more likely, is an intelligent creator behind the human DNA, the colossal biological database that contains no fewer than 3.5 billion "letters"? No, we are not a random mass of molecules that was produced by a mindless process.

Despots

However, why is atheism and its' Siamese twin, evolution, so dangerous to young minds? It is because evolutionary – atheistic philosophy puts despots in power who devastate society. It is no wonder that despots like Joseph Stalin and Adolph Hitler could deliberately kill so many millions of people and have no conscience about it. They saw man as just another higher form of animal life, and therefore there is no accountability to a living, creating God. Paul describes this kind as people who have their conscience seared with a hot iron. (I Timothy 4: 2)

Fallout

The Fallout from Darwinian Evolution has been abhorrent, loathsome, and repugnant. It has led to a monstrous thing called Social Darwinism, as mentioned earlier. This means that the philosophy of Darwin (and that is all it has ever been-**not science**) must be used in every facet of society. For instance, in America there are legal minds who say that the Constitution must **evolve**. It must be a "living document." It must change according to the whims of the times. They feel that the great principles upon which this nation was founded and upon which it became the most amazing government on the face of the earth, must be abandoned and that we must live under the tyranny of the 51%. That means that if 51% of the Germans supported Hitler, he had a perfect right to kill the Jews. They contend that whatever the 51% want as public policy at any given time must be done. That is what they call democracy! However, our pledge of allegiance affirms that we "pledge allegiance to the flag of the United States of America and to the **Republic** for which it stands ..." A republic is the rule by majority with the **rights of the minority protected**. That is the way America was founded.

Academic Freedom?

In America, academic freedom or the freedom of inquiry has been a sacred thing to us but the Darwinists in the educational sector of America have **swept it aside**. For instance, it was Ben Stein in his documentary concerning **Intelligent Design** who pointed out ways in which academic freedom has been **shackled** in this nation. He pointed out that Dr. **Richard Von Sternberg** was pressured to resign at the Smithsonian Institute because he gave publicity to an article on **Intelligent Design**. This happened in spite of favorable peer review. He was viewed as an "intellectual terrorist." Dr. **Caroline Crocker** lost her job at the esteemed George Mason University because she dared to talk about **Intelligent Design**. Similarly, at Baylor University, Dr. **Robert J. Marks II** was forced to shut down his website and return grant money because he talked about **Intelligent Design** (Baylor was founded by devout Baptists). Stein also pointed out that at Iowa State, Dr. **Guillermo Gonzales** was denied tenure because he dared to talk about Intelligent Design, which is simply the belief that there was an **intelligence behind the creation of the Universe**. Stein pointed out that there were many more **who would not allow themselves to be identified** for fear of reprisal. **How did we get to that!** In the film, Stein interviewed Richard Dawkins, the notorious atheist who wrote the slanderous and vituperative book called "The God Delusion." Dawkins admitted that evolution had **driven him toward atheism**. When Ben Stein pressed him about how life began to start with, he simply obfuscated. When Stein pressed him hard enough, he admitted that there could have been some highly intelligent form of life somewhere in the **eons** past that could have created life, as we know it. So, in the end, he had no other explanation other than that there was some kind of superior intelligence behind the universe. Christians know him as **Jehovah God**, as revealed in the Bible.

In earlier days, the evolutionists claimed **academic freedom** in order to gain the right to present their evolutionary nonsense but now they want to **deny that same right** to others who disagree with them and believe that there is intelligence behind the **design of the universe**.

Evolution Discredited

Darwin hung his entire theory on a process he described as "natural selection" which Herbert Spencer later referred to as "survival of the fittest." Darwin's theory was that there were times in the past when there had been **upward trans-mutations**. No one has ever observed one. There has **never** been **any evidence** to support it and every experience of man has been that mutations are **always downward** and **not upward**. The survival of the fittest has always been nonsense. Nothing was "fitter" than the **Dinosaur**s but they **did not survive** while the lowly cockroach and grasshoppers, or locusts, **did survive**. The evolutionists like to claim that Dinosaurs existed millions and millions of years ago but that too is false. In fact, the book of Job describes Dinosaurs in the 40th and 41st chapters. Some believe that the stories about Dragons found in folklore, all the way from China to England, came from Dinosaurs.

Fallback Position

The fallback argument of the evolutionist has been that adaptation demonstrated evolution. That, too, is bucolic **nonsense**. An evolutionist this writer met once tried to demonstrate that some kangaroos with slightly variant shapes in their ears gave evidence of evolution. Of course, it did not because they were **still kangaroos**. There has never been any **evidence** whatever that one species has ever become another species. There has never been any evidence whatever that an orangutan, somewhere along the line, became a human. The so-called "transitional species," or what is commonly referred to as "the missing link," has never been found among all the thousands and thousands of fossils that men have examined. In fact, neither Darwin nor any of his successors have ever been able to define precisely what a species is. They have never been able to say how life **started to begin with**. They only deal with what they **think** happened after life came into existence. Science has to have credible evidence and Evolutionists have never been able to supply that credible evidence, nor has it ever been observed. It has **never** moved beyond the realm of **hypothesis**.

Final Blow

The discovery of the DNA template removed **all credibility** from the evolutionary **hypothesis**. DNA scientists have discovered that a single DNA molecule contains incomprehensible amounts of information. One cell contains more information than could be found in an entire set of the Encyclopedia Britannica. Only an intelligent God could do that. Some scientists call DNA "the language of life." Others refer to it as "the most golden of all molecules." These cells are found to be so complex and so accurate in replication that a transitional species would be impossible. Robert T. Clark and James D. Bales wrote a book about "**Why Scientists Accept Evolution**." They show that Darwin, Huxley, Spencer and other early evolutionists did not start in that direction because of science or evidence but because of emotional and spiritual **bias against God, the Bible, and Christianity**. It was from this prejudicial belief system that they interpreted whatever meager "evidence" they thought they had in favor of a materialistic explanation of matter. Evolution became their substitute for God. Dr. Bolton Davidheiser was an evolutionist for many years. He received a PHD at John Hopkins University. His specialty was genetics. As he studied genetics, he turned **from** evolution **to** Christianity. Dr. James F. Coppedge describes Davidheiser's first book "**Evolution and Christian Faith**" as one of the most complete and scholarly studies yet about those who make the subject of evolution into a **type of religion**.

Mentality

A very devious, disconcerting mentality has crept across America in recent years. It is the idea that we just must believe, as Frances Schaeffer pointed out, the "men in the white coats" (scientists). Many Americans believe that they are all studious, prima-diligent searchers for truth and that they are totally objective. This was not true of Darwin and his friends as we have already demonstrated and it is not true today. Scientists have bias, prejudice, and narrow mindedness just like any other profession. One thing every student learns early in the study of philosophy is that there is no such thing as **total objectivity**. There are hundreds and hundreds of illustrations across this country proving that there are times when science cannot only be wrong, but destructive and harmful. Several years ago there was a drug called Thalidomide. It was heralded as a tremendous breakthrough for expectant mothers who were experiencing difficulty but alas, it was found to cause terrible birth defects and had to be removed from the market. This kind of thing could be illustrated hundreds of times over, not only in the field of pharmacy, but in the field of medicine. How many times have well-intentioned social programs caused "unintended consequences" that actually did more harm than good.

Narrow Minded Scientists

James F. Coppedge in his book quotes James Watson, who discovered the pairing mechanism of DNA, said, "In contrast to the popular conception supported by newspapers and mothers of scientists, a goodly number of scientists are not only **narrow minded** and **dull** but also **stupid**." While this is not true of most scientists, there is certainly that element among **some of those** in the field of science. Coppedge points out that there is a great variety of beliefs, attitudes and character among scientists just as there is among politicians, teachers, and salespersons. Some **evolutionists** become crusaders for their viewpoint, which is often rooted in **anti-God fanaticism**. There are other scientists who simply "go along to get along" with it while others gladly echo it. Others have serious doubts about evolution but they keep quiet about it. Then, of course, many are honestly confused about the question. Some believe, not because of **real evidence**, but **because of presumed evidence** and this has a great deal to do with the prevalence of evolutionary thought in our day. John G. Read, an aerospace engineer, and a former evolutionist himself, said: "I regard evolution as a **major myth** of our time - a **myth** in the name of **science**."

William Randolph Hearst Jr. once described the pressures of "fashionable ideas which are advanced with such force that **common sense itself becomes the victim**." A person under such pressure may act, "with an **irrationality** which is almost **beyond belief**." That is a perfect description of the overwhelming pressure upon educators to accept evolution without question. The sad thing is that many who profess faith in Jesus Christ, our Lord, shy away from any confrontation with the **destructive, anti-God myth of evolution**. George Charles Roche III said, "Modern man does not seem to understand that science can harbor illusions on the image of nature and thus **mislead**."

No Answers

The fact is that evolution does not provide answers to the most basic questions of life. Evolution cannot tell us how life began. Without **upward mutations,** evolution is **dead**. As pointed out earlier, this just never happens. Mutations are always downward. Yes, there are ways that breeders breed for certain characteristics in cattle, horses and other animals and there are certain heritable traits in humans but that does not demonstrate evolution **at all**! These **variations** come **within species**. There has never been any proof whatever that one species has evolved into another species. In fact, as pointed out earlier, evolution has never even been able to describe what a **species** is. As B'Nei Hamelech well put it, "It is critical for us to understand that without a personal creator God, without any external, objective truth, eventually we are left with a universe that is the product of nothing but impersonal time plus chance." Even Charles Darwin, the father of the evolution heresy, recognized the difficulty in explaining the universe in terms of time and chance when he wrote in his autobiography, "With my mind I cannot believe that these things come by chance." In other places, he wrote of his own theories, "I know in my mind that this can't be true, but my mind is only a monkey's mind and who can trust a mind like that?" In fact, it was demonstrated years ago that all matter is of the same age.

The explosion of information concerning the human genome in recent years has been overwhelming and has presented positive proof that all creatures reproduce "according to its kind" (Genesis 1: 24 - 25).

Obstacles

There are huge, overwhelming scientific obstacles that evolution has never been able to address. One is the second law of thermodynamics. This law, which is observable and demonstrable, simply says that everything goes from **order to disorder**. Evolution, however, contends that all matter goes from **disorder to order.** Entropy is at work in the universe and in all living things. That is the reason that we look older every year that we live. It affects all of creation. Even the hardest of stones will finally degrade when exposed to the atmosphere as can be easily observed out in the painted deserts of the Southwest or in any old cemetery. There is no credible way to reverse that process even though humans sometimes try facelifts and all kinds of skin treatment. The second law is never reversed and the Bible says it clearly: *"It is appointed unto man once to die and after that the judgment."* (Hebrews 9:27) The second law helps us to understand the truth of that law and no one ever cheats that law. When sin came into the world through Adam, the **entire creation** fell and Adam would earn his living by the sweat of his face (Genesis 3: 17-24).

Age of the Universe

There is **no reason** for the geological ages that are touted by the evolutionists, except to give time to accommodate **evolution**. It is nothing more than an accommodation to the evolutionists. The mantra of the evolutionist is **radio-metric dating**. The most common method of this kind of dating is the carbon 14 (C^{14}) method. For many years, this method was touted as indisputable for determining the age of matter. Alas, it has been found to be almost totally unreliable. It has **some** usefulness in determining young dates. The system was developed by Dr. Willard F. Libby for which he received the Nobel Prize. Dr. Melvin A. Cook, who received his PhD in physical chemistry at Yale, provides extensive discussion of the techniques of radiocarbon dating. He states, **"There really are no reliable time clocks."** He makes this statement in spite of all the contrary opinions that have been advanced. Dr. Coppedge quotes from an article by Professor Robert L. Whitelaw, a nuclear consultant at Virginia Polytechnic Institute, who stated his opinion that "cosmic rays" may have accounted altogether for the buildup of argon 36, which is, as he phrased it, "well within the 7,000 years since Biblical creation."

About the Long Age Concept

Froelich Rainey said, concerning the carbon 14 method, "Unfortunately the difficulties and complexities in arriving at a **'true' date for any event by this method are not clear**... Many archaeologists still think of radiocarbon dating as a scientific technique that must be right or wrong. **Would that it was so simple.**" He points out that "1870 BC is the earliest actual recorded date in human history." Dr. Coppedge states that few people really realize how much uncertainty is involved in dates prior to that. Dr. Melvin A. Cook, using an exact application of

Libby's method for carbon 14 dating finds the atmosphere to be about 10,000 years of age. In addition, Dr. Cook, discussing the uranium-thorium-lead process arrives at different conclusions that **dispute** the standard **long age concept**. Evolutionists tend to ignore the tests that reveal **short term** dating of the universe and results that do not match their **pre-conceived ideas**. It is surprising to find that there is strong evidence that the **Mississippi River** may be only about **5,000 years old**; using evidence based on a geological study of the Mississippi Delta. Another shocker is that modern measurements have discovered that the average Neanderthal and Cro-Magnon men have considerably larger brain capacity than modern man, which certainly obliterates the theories concerning the evolution of man. For instance, the so-called "cave man" posture of the Neanderthal man as pictured in magazines and newspapers is without foundation. Dr. Coppedge directs us to the *Encyclopedia Britannica* of 1967, which gave this explanation:

"**The popular conception that these people were slouched in posture and walked with a shuffling knee bent gait seems to have been due in large part to the faulty re-construction of the skull base and the misinterpretation of certain features of the limb bones of one of the Neanderthal skeletons discovered early in the 20th Century.**"

It is often true that the dramatic claims of evolutionists are often withdrawn later but the withdrawal **seldom ever makes the news**.

Your Decision

Space will not permit the discussion of the labyrinthine of details concerning human genetics and DNA. Suffice it to say that we have covered enough of the material to assure the reader that evolution is not scientific but it is a philosophy that has been thoroughly discredited in the scientific field. While evolution **cannot** explain the **beginning of life**, God does explain it in His Word in both the Old and New Testaments and it is totally reliable and trustworthy. The **Word of God** is truth, without any mixture of error. Good science has never disproved the Scripture but rather reaffirms it. Archaeological discoveries have simply **amplified** our understanding of the Word of God. The Apostle John has given double assurance in his Gospel and his first Epistle that the triune **God** is behind it all. The words of both John and Jesus have reaffirmed that Jesus was active in creation and that the Genesis account of Creation is absolutely true. The only question modern man has to decide is whether he will believe the postulants of an ill-trained pseudo-scientist of the 19th century named Charles Darwin or will he believe the Word of God and the clear teachings of Jesus Christ, the Son of God, and the Savior of the world. As for me and my house, I choose Jesus and the Word of God because He was the **Living Word**. Many books have been written about human genetics and DNA science which, with graphs and illustrations, demonstrate again and again that all living things are replicated *"according to its kind."* (Genesis 1: 24-25) There is no need for our young people to be confused about evolutionary nonsense any more.

Why Does It Continue?

We have seen that evolution is a bankrupt philosophy. So, why is it still around? It is still around because some want a universe **without God**! However, such a view not only is contrary to Scripture, but it flies in the face of all reason. The **cosmological**, **teleological**, and **ontological** theses for the existence of a living God plus honest scientific revelations (such as DNA) provide abounding empirical evidence that there is a living God behind creation and that evolution is little more than capricious blather that provides **no meaning to anything** and promotes nothing but **doubt and confusion**.

The Cosmological Evidences

The cosmological evidences for the existence of a living God were associated with Thomas Aquinas. It is simply a reference to the world around us. His four assertions by which he supports the cosmological evidences are:

1. Since motion exists, there must be a cause for that motion. Since there is a first **cause,** there has to be a first source, which is moved and can be moved by nothing else. All men understand that source to be the living God.

2. Since movements are caused, every event that occurs in nature has a condition, which precedes it in time. That is known as the efficient cause. This is the idea that the cause of the cause has a cause, etc. Such endless regression finally ends in infinite nothingness since it never explains anything.

3. Since contingent things exist, a necessary being, which is the living God, must be recognized.

4. Since varying degrees of perfection exist, an infinitely perfect being must be recognized.

Natural Accountability

These recognitions reveal that both change and existence must be accounted for. God's nature is inferred from outward facts in the order of nature such as motion, change, and development. Simply put we can say, "Someone had to make everything else, so someone had to make the world." The argument runs as follows:

1. Every event has a cause.
2. The universe is an event.
3. Therefore, the universe has a cause.
4. That cause is the living God because there had to be intelligence behind it all.

It is obvious then, that the cosmological evidences for the existence of God rejects the Darwinian nonsensical argument of a self-producing universe or the self-generation of humankind. The cosmological evidences also reject the Darwinian ideas that adaptation equals evolution or those variations within a species equals evolution. Instead, the cosmologist embraces the Biblical principle that, "God made the beast of the earth **after his kind** and cattle **after their kind** and everything that creepeth upon the earth **after his kind** and God saw that it was good." (Genesis 1: 24-25) Of course, Darwin lived long before the explosion of information concerning the human genome, a study of which has made it firm and clear that both the plant and animal kingdom produce **after their kind**! There has never been any evidence presented by the Darwinian fanatical nonsense that there has ever been the evolving of one species into a different species.

Sane people must admit to the existence of the world of nature. It stands as its' own proof. If there is the existence of the world of nature, there is a cause and the cause beyond nature is the living God unless we are to rest in an ultimate inexplicability of our world and surrender the idea of any attempt to frame an intelligent conception of nature at all. The cosmological argument demonstrates the existence of God beyond all rational doubt and, in fact, it is much more intelligent indeed than any alternative hypothesis about the world's existence.

At Lystra

Paul employed the cosmological argument more than once. While at Lystra, he came upon a lame man. When he saw that the lame man had faith to be healed of his infirmity, Paul commanded him to stand to his feet and he did. As a result, the people concluded that the gods had come down among them and they worshipped Paul and Barnabas. They wanted to call Barnabas Jupiter and Paul Mercurius because Paul was the chief speaker. Paul and Barnabas resisted this attempt to make them into pagan gods so much that they rent their clothes and ran in among the people crying out, *"Sirs, why do you do these things? We also are men of like passions with you, and preach unto you that you should turn from these vanities unto the living God, which made heaven, and earth, and sea, and all things that are therein."* He further pointed out that God, *"**left not Himself without witness** in that He did **good**, and gave us **rain** from heaven, and **fruitful seasons**, filling our hearts with **food and gladness**."* (Acts 14: 8-17) Without a doubt, Paul here is pointing out that the existence of a living God is self-evident in nature and the world around them and that their lives were not so blessed by such pagan gods as Jupiter and Mercurius.

Intuitive Knowledge

The most powerful use of the cosmological evidence is found in Romans 1: 18 – 32. This passage points out that the **wrath of God is revealed from heaven** against all ungodliness and unrighteousness of men. He points out that they **hold the truth of God** in **unrighteousness.**

He further points out that men are guilty because, *"That which may be **known** of God is manifested **in them** for God hath **showed** it unto them."* He further points out that the invisible things from the creation of the world are clearly seen, being **understood** by the **things that are made**, even by His eternal power and God-head so that man is **without excuse**. What Paul is pointing out here is that because of the evidence in creation it is quite clear that man can clearly understand from the **things that are made**, the eternal power, and Godhead. He is pointing out that there is an intuitive knowledge of God in man, which cannot be ignored but can be known by simply observing what God has created. From the very time of creation, man has known God. However, the drifting away from God into idolatry was the choice that man freely made and when they knew God they **glorified Him not as God** nor were they thankful. They became vain in their imaginations and, as a result, their **foolish hearts were darkened**.

Human Foolishness

In their human wisdom, they professed to be wise and they brought forth human ideas that made them **fools**. Instead of worshipping and serving God, they *"changed the glory of the incorruptible God into an image made like corruptible man."* They began to worship **things** of nature instead of the **God** of nature. They were **driven by lusts** of their own hearts. This led to dishonoring their **own bodies between themselves**. Paul points out that this arrogant **vanity** of men **caused** men, while professing themselves to be **wise**, to become **fools**. They changed the incorruptible God into an image made like **corruptible man** as well as fowls and beasts and other creeping things. As a result, God **gave them up** or abandoned them to uncleanliness through their **own lusts** and they thus **dishonored** their **own bodies between themselves**.

Paul further points out that homosexuality is the ultimate distortion of God's creative genius and that homosexuality is antithetical to the truth and purpose of God in that man began to serve and worship creatures more than the creator. As they **denied God**, He gave them up to **vile affection** that ended in women doing things that are unnatural and men burning in their lusts one toward another, *"Men with men working that which is unseemly and receiving in **themselves** that **recompense** of their error** which was mete."* In other words, terrible, debilitating, and often fatal diseases are the result of such vile affections and immoral behavior. Therefore, homosexuals can never say, "God made me this way." God did no such thing! Homosexuality is an acquired behavior that results from vile affections for which God **cannot be blamed**. It is blasphemous to say such things.. A study of homosexuals taking part in ministries affiliated with Exodus Intentional, the nation's largest ministry devoted to helping homosexuals out of that lifestyle, have found that many of them do **change** to a heterosexual orientation. However, this wonderful liberating change will **never take place** as long as churches tell them that they are "just fine" and that they are "OK" with God.

They chose **not to retain God** in their knowledge and God gave them over to a **reprobate mind** to do those things, which are not convenient. The word **reprobate** is translated from the Greek word adokimos (αδοκιμος). It signifies something that **does not stand the test** and is **rejected**. Thus, the reprobate mind is a mind whose thought processes have been rejected by God because they refused to have God in their knowledge. Paul writes about it in his second letter to Timothy concerning those who are *"**reprobate concerning the faith**."* (II Timothy 3: 8)

End Product

Paul is making it clear that when one rejects all the evidences of God that are around him he has become so vile in his nature that he commits all kinds of sin that his mind can imagine while all the time claiming that he is too wise to believe the Word of God or the existence of God. The kind of persons described by Paul is now rampant in America. Many persons who commit such **indecent** things often pawn themselves off on us as "Christians." Yet they participate in every vile thing they can imagine, including homosexuality. Some churches have **compromised at this point**. Such people represent themselves as being "too smart" or "too wise" to embrace the **plain teachings of the Word of God** and every evidence in our world that there is a real and living God whom we will one day stand before to give an account of our lives as Jesus pointed out in His teachings. When a church gives in and **compromises** with these vile practices and affections, then that church has lost its' power and has no reason to exist but these are the kinds of things that men drift into when they reject the **teachings of** or **beliefs in** the living God and all the evidence about Him that surrounds us. Some churches are now performing homosexual marriages and allowing homosexuals to hold office in the church. Adulterous unions in which men and women simply start living together without marriage are becoming all too frequent among many who claim to be **Christians**. It later causes many legal and emotional problems and produces children who are confused about family relationships. It is little wonder that so **many** of those churches are **declining**. These things happen because man chooses **not to retain God** in his reasoning! This sort of conduct is a product of **atheism.** That is exactly what Paul is pointing out.

The Teleological Evidence

The **teleological** evidence for the existence of God is known today as the belief in **intelligent design.** It simply means that everything in the universe is created toward a purpose, including inorganic matter. It applies to both the plant and animal kingdoms. Everything trends to move toward a **purpose** or an end. For instance, every organ in the human body has a purpose. We have learned that through surgery some parts of the body can be removed and we can still live but the function of the human body is diminished by that much. The best evidence of this is what the biologists call the "**balance of nature**." In other words, everything is designed for some purpose, which leads to the existence of an intelligent designer, which we know, is the **living God**.

The Philosophers

This philosophy of religion was developed from Greek thinking, which has morphed into modern thinking. Socrates developed the proof of purposeful design and even assigned to it a definite **theistic** reference. Plato and Aristotle both advanced versions of the teleological postulate which points to **God** as the **originator of the universe** even though Plato's "ideal" city was little more than a caste system. Thomas Aquinas advanced this belief during the medieval period. He insisted that things, which lack intelligence, such as natural bodies, move toward an end or a **purpose**. This is evident from their acting consistently as to obtain the **best results**. He insisted that it is not fortuitously, but designedly, that the elements act to achieve their end. Whatever lacks intelligence cannot move toward an end or a purpose unless it is directed toward such an end by some being endowed with intelligence. Therefore, there has to be some intelligent being who acts upon the natural universe and directs everything to its' purposeful end and this being is the **living God**.

Wolf and Paley who were great admirers of Thomas Aquinas used this thesis very forcefully during the 18th and 19th centuries. They contended that inorganic phenomena in the natural order operate in terms of **ends** and that the natural world does not behave in an orderly fashion simply by chance but because of a **deliberate intention by a living God**.

The Opposite View

In 1859 Charles Darwin published a work called "Origin of Species" which took the **opposite view** and introduced a disconnect in the thinking of man inferring that all of these things took place by **chance**. For thousands of years men had lived with the assurance of **fixity**, especially in the western mind, but Darwin introduced the amphigoric idea of **flux** in everything. The result of his deranged thinking was that it posited a natural view of the origin of nature and man, tending to turn man away from a belief in the existence of God as a basis of the plainly observable design and purpose in the universe by a living God. He tended to replace the prevailing assumption of the **permanency** of species reproduction and order of nature with the concept of **change by chance**. Some even contended that his doctrine of natural selection had destroyed the cogency of the teleological evidence for the existence of God by showing that changes have come by purely natural causes rather than by special design. However, this is by no means evident today nor has it **ever** been evident.

There are some very deep and relevant questions that Darwin leaves unanswered such as:

1. The problems of **gaps** or "**missing links**" between lower forms of life and man.
2. The failure of Darwin to account for the **arrival** of the fittest.
3. The failure of Darwin to account for the **law of variables** and its limits.
4. His inability to account for how **small variations** could remain until the time for a "new species" to develop.

5. His failure to explain human beings apart from the **image of God in man**.

Order and Beauty

There is still order and beauty in nature. The earth is unique in providing the conditions that make life possible. The inorganic world seems to be a preparation in which the lower stages of the organic development appear as a support for the higher.

F. R. Tenent demonstrates that the Christian worldview is the most logical and probable of all world explanations from the standpoint of objective reasonableness rather than subjective certitude. He offered five features of the real world that demand a Christian worldview as the only plausible and reasonable explanation. They are:

1. The fact that the real world is **stable** and related – not chaotic.
2. The world shows a progressive **arrival of the fit.**
3. The **order** of inorganic adaptations of living organisms. He affirms that hosts of factors, astronomical, thermal, chemical, etc., which are not causally related, have merged to make an environment, which is **fitted** for living organisms to **survive**. It is **not credible** or **sensible** that this should be an ungrounded coincident of compounded chemical particles.
4. The fact that **nature** invokes **beauty** in man's consciousness.
5. The fact that nature is an order **instrumental** to **morality**.

As we can see then, a **Christian worldview** becomes more exacting when these **lines** of **fact** are taken in their interconnectedness. The dovetailing of these several fields of fact that are not directly related speaks loudly of an intelligent **design** by an intelligent **Being**, whom we know as **God**, and who worked on a **cosmic scale**!

Ontological Evidence

The ontological evidence for the existence of a living God boils down to the **image of God in man**. It harks back to Genesis 1: 26 (KJV) in which God said, "...*let us make man in our image, after our likeness: and let them have dominion over the fish of the sea, and over the fowl of the air, and over the cattle, and over all the earth, and over every creeping thing that creepeth upon the earth.*" There was a distinct difference between man and the animal kingdom. Therefore, God gave man dominion over the animal kingdom. The ontological evidence for the existence of God is the existence of God in the mind of man. Since God exists to some extent in the mind of man and **He is a being of whom there cannot be a greater one imagined or conceived**, He is a being who exists in **fact** and not merely in thought and He is greater than a being that could exist only in thought. The ontological evidence for the existence of God is closely associated with Augustine whom many consider the greatest figure, other than Jesus and the Apostles, in the formative history of Christian thought.

Ontology says, I know that I exist. That is self-evident. I also know that there was a time when I did not exist. I do not exist independently of the world in which I live. I know that I was not self-generated. I know that some outside force working through very exacting and dependable laws of life and existence brought me into existence. I know that there has been a process of development within me that was and is governed by extremely minute but tremendously powerful genes. I know that other things and other beings exist and that they, like me, are **limited** and **finite**. Thus, I understand that this very complex but exacting process is controlled by some being that is both an **unlimited** and **infinite** being and that being is the living **God. It did not happen by chance,** as the Darwinians would have you believe because Darwin's thinking was irrational.

Reality

We are talking about a living God who exists not only in man's mind but in reality and the very **existence** of man **declares** that reality. The image of God in man makes man a special creation. He is not a part of the animal kingdom. He is not like animals. He is created in the **image** of **God.** Man has the ability to do complex thinking, which animals do not have; they only have instincts. An animal can be **trained** but cannot be **educated** to do complex thinking or perform complicated tasks. For instance, evolutionists contend that man evolved from primates but one can go into the habitats of primates and they live like they have lived for thousands of years. They do not construct such things as shelters or tools. They cannot perform such simple tasks as making a fire or cooking. There is no resemblance to man who has developed a world of technology. If there was ever a transition from primates to man it would still happen **but it does not.**

Man has the ability to communicate through language far above any communication that comes naturally to any member of the animal kingdom. These things constitute the inviolable proof of the **image of God in man!** Existence is perfection. An existence in the mind is not perfection but existence in **reality is perfection.** Of course, man realizes that he is imperfect and his salvation comes through trust and belief in a **perfect being** who is the **Son of the living God.** In fact, **that** God exists and **what** God **is** are actually one. Anselm contended that God is not known **through** nature but that nature is known **in** God. To Anselm, it was only **rational** to believe in a living God and was **irrational** to

75

believe that there is no living God. Moreover, because God is a **reality,** we can **communicate** with God through **prayer**.

The Mind and Intellect

The ontological postulation concerning the existence of God is grounded explicitly in Biblical testimony. Man is not required to suppress his **intellect** or dismiss his **mind** in his seeking for God. For instance, the Apostle Paul has much to say about the foolishness of human wisdom in which human thinking makes a man foolish. (Romans 1: 21-22). We are not required to set aside our **minds** but rather to **engage** our **minds** in our understanding of God and His creation. This is never more clear than what we find in Romans 12 where the Apostle said, *"I beseech you therefore, brethren, by the mercies of God, that you present yourselves a **living sacrifice,** holy, acceptable unto God, which is your **reasonable** service and be not conformed to this world: but be ye **transformed** by the **renewing of your mind** that you may **prove** what is that **good**, and **acceptable**, and **perfect**, will of God."* (Romans 12: 1-2) Yes, God expects us to employ our **reason** in understanding Him and His ways.

When Paul is explaining to the Philippians that Christ was a part of the Godhead he said, *"Let this **mind** be in you which was also in **Christ Jesus:** who being in the **form of God,** thought it not robbery to be equal with God: but made of Himself no reputation, and took upon Him the **form** of a **servant** and was made in the **likeness of men:** and being found in **fashion** as a **man**, He humbled Himself, and became obedient unto death, even the death of the cross."* (Philippians 2: 5-8) Therefore, we see then, that the exercise of the mind is integral to the understanding of God and of the Trinity. We see also, that God has **form** and in Christ, we can **understand** something of that form.

The Soul of Man

The things we have discussed above lead us directly and logically to the consideration concerning the soul of man. God created man from the dust of the earth and *"breathed into his nostrils the breath of life; and man became a living soul."* (Genesis 2: 7) This is not said of any species of the animal kingdom. It is only said of **man**. The Hebrew word is *nephesh*. It is sometimes translated as "life" but it is translated "soul" 428 times. We are now discussing a very, very important truth of Christianity that is very basic to our understanding of the words and ways of God. The Atheists often contend that unless something can be perceived by the five senses, it is not real. To them, that is **reality**, but it is a false premise. The most important characteristic of a human **cannot** be perceived through the five senses (taste, touch, smell, hear, see). There is a great, unimaginable gulf between the animal kingdom and humankind. That is the reason well informed Christians have always rejected the Darwinian hypothesis that humans evolved from lower animal life. Animals are not living souls. Man, however, is a **living soul**. That is what the **image of God in man** is all about. We have discussed the characteristics of humans such as the ability to do complex thinking, reasoning and acquiring skills with which they can learn, build, travel, and perform complicated tasks.

The most real thing about any human is their brain function. As has been pointed out, animals only respond to external stimuli but a human can reason. A human has thought processes. No one can see, taste, touch, hear, or smell a thought. Yet, it is the most important thing about the existence of man. When one's thought processes cease the doctor will examine that individual and either pronounce him dead or in a vegetative state. This is when the soul of man departs and enters the heavenly abode if that soul has

77

been saved by trusting Jesus and His sacrifice at Calvary for our sin..

God, in His boundless love, has decreed a plan of salvation for man because man is created in the image of God. The provision of salvation was *"foreordained before the foundation of the world."* (I Peter 1: 20) Thus, we understand that once human life is created by the living God, there will never be a time when that life does not exist because it will continue through eternity. For the one who chooses life through Jesus Christ, there will be a place for that soul in Heaven as John made it abundantly clear in the 14th Chapter of his Gospel. It is also made clear that the person who rejects Jesus Christ will be conscious and personal forever throughout eternity but his abode will be in an eternal Hell. (Luke 16: 19-31) Jesus said it well when He said, *"He that believeth on Him is not condemned: but He that believeth not is **condemned already, because he hath not believed in the name of the only begotten Son of God.**"* (John 3: 18) Eternal Hell is a place that is beyond human description because it is so terrible. However, the wonderful news is that Jesus has made a way of salvation so that no one has to go to that terrible place where there is no joy, happiness, peace, or contentment. We see, then, that the soul of man is an imprint of the image of God in man and that the most important thing about any human individual is that which cannot be perceived through the five senses. Yet, it is more **real** than anything else about us and thus, God saw something in us worth redeeming.

Now we understand that those divinely inspired words of Paul in Romans 12: 1-2, are telling us that knowing God is **transformational**. The word he uses is **metamorphoō** (μεταμορφόω). Our word **metamorphosis** comes from it. It really means to change into another entity. He is really saying that just as surely as that ugly worm changes into a beautiful butterfly through a process that is always true under every circumstance and is immutable, so the individual who comes to the triune God, fully embracing Him, changes from a state of death unto a state of life (John 5: 24). That process is always teleologically perfect. It is dependable and it never changes. It is one of God's divine laws of life. It is a planned and orderly process that has been set in motion from the foundation of the world by a living God! It is a process that is understandable by **finite** man and comes from an **infinite** living God. Again, it is **never** by chance but this transformation brings about a **renewing of the mind** which brings about right thinking. This is the reason **well informed** Christians have traditionally rejected the Evolutionary Hypothesis. It does violence to the most basic truth of Christianity and indeed, to civilization as a whole, that man is a **special divine creation** by the very **God of creation**. This is not and can never be true of animals or their **progeny**. It is, therefore, literally impossible that man could have evolved from animals which have no soul into a human who was a direct and unique creation of God in God's own image. This is the reason that evolution is **totally wrong**. It is, moreover, a blatant blasphemy of God's creation and has no kinship whatever to **propositional truth**! We will discuss this further in Chapter 3.

John's Writing

All of these theses by which we come to know about our development as finite beings, are also revealed in the writings of John. It is John who reminds us *"In the **beginning** was the **word** and the **word** was with **God**, and the word **was God**. The same was in the **beginning** with **God**. All things were **made by Him**; and without Him was not **anything ma**de that was **made**."* (John 1: 1-3 KJV) John makes it clear that Jesus was a part of the triune Godhead and that He was active in creation but John does not stop there. He makes it clear that Jesus was the *"true light, which* *lighteth **every man** that cometh into the world."* (John 1: 9) As stated before, no man is without some divine light. Paul made the same association in Romans 1. John also made it clear that this divine light was knowable or that the truth of God was knowable because *"He was made flesh and dwelt among us, and we **beheld His glory**, the glory as of the only begotten of the Father, full of grace and truth."* (John 1: 14 KJV) John was an **eyewitness**! He was there at Jesus' transfiguration. (Matthew 17: 1-13) He really had **beheld His glory**! It was not some mysterious secret thing.

When Paul was arraigned before Festus and Agrippa in Acts 26, Festus tried the same trick that the cynical world always tries. He charged Paul with being "mad." The Greek word that Festus used was **mania** (μανια). Our word "maniac" is a derivative word. Paul was giving testimony of his conversion and was asserting that Agrippa **knew** what he was saying to be true because *"none of these things are hidden from him; for this thing was **not done in a corner**."* (Acts 26: 26 KJV) Atheists often ask the question as to why God is so "secretive" about His existence if, indeed, He does exist. Paul's answer is that He definitely is **not** secretive. The mighty works of God are plainly visible and are there for any honest seeker to see and understand. **It was not done in a corner**!

The Eternal God/Man

John points out that **John the Baptist** also bore witness of Him and stated clearly that He was **before** John the Baptist even though John the Baptist was chronologically older than Jesus (John 1: 15). Why did John refer to Him as **the word**? Because words **communicate** and John is saying, that Jesus Christ was God's **ultimate communication** of the **image of God** in man. It is in Jesus Christ that we understand **who** God is and **what** He is like. He also declared, *"... the **only begotten Son**, which is in the bosom* *of the Father, He hath **declared Him**.*" Yes, we can understand more of the living God because **His Son**, Jesus Christ, came to reveal Him to us. Jesus, Himself, declared, "*He that hath **seen Me** hath **seen the Father** ...*" Seven hundred years before Jesus was born Isaiah declared that Jesus would be born miraculously of a virgin and that His name would be called **Emmanuel** which means "**God with us**." (Isaiah 7: 14 KJV) Jesus also announced to His disciples that the mighty works He performed were empowered by the **Father** when He said, "*... **He doeth the works**.*" He also taught His disciples that if they had trouble in believing in the living God, that the mighty works He did **proclaimed the living God** when He said, "*Believe Me that I am in the Father and the Father in Me, or else believe Me for the very **works** sake.*" (John 14: 9-11 KJV) Peter made this point on the day of Pentecost when he declared that Jesus was "*approved of God among you by **miracles and wonders** and **signs** which **God** did by **Him** ...*" (Acts 2: 22 KJV) Nicodemus was persuaded that **Jesus** came from **God** because of the fact that "*...no **man** can do these **miracles**...except **God** be with him.*" (John 3: 2 KJV) It was John, more than any other New Testament writer or any philosopher of his age who stressed the miracles of Jesus as the authentication and confirmation of the fact that He was no **ordinary** man but that He was the **God/man**.

Yes, we can know God and we can know His existence even better through His Son, Jesus Christ. However, the best evidence for a living God is a **life lived**! Understanding this, we still must "*...walk by **faith**, not by **sight**.*" (II Corinthians 5: 7 KJV)

Academic Freedom?

We have illustrated how evolutionary swill has poisoned the minds of our youth and has incited despicable and devastating social policies that have oppressed people wherever evolution has gone. We have also illustrated that God's creation can easily

81

be known by man when he honestly employs his reason and intellect. In America, however, the freedom of speech and academic freedom are being **denied** faculty members and students in the schools and colleges of this nation by **sinister** and **cynical** evolutionists in **places** of **power**.

Self-Generation Fallacy

Any reasonable and sensible person, even of average intelligence, will know that self-generation of life never takes place now and never has. If natural elements or compounds coming together by chance could produce life, it would **still be happening** but it **never happens** even with the intelligence of a scientist guiding the process. There had to be a living God behind it all. The Bible makes it clear that God created man from the dust of the earth but only **He could do it** (Genesis 2: 7). Scientists have tried and tried to create human life in a test tube but it has never worked. One scientist who even thought he could re-create dinosaurs from DNA found in dinosaur skeletons, but it never happened. Charles Darwin, himself, said that the intricacies of the human eye gave him "cold shudders." Why? Because it debunked his theory. An Ophthalmologist told this writer that a normal human eye contains "about two million optic fibers." That kind of thing does not happen by **chance**! Even today, evolutionists prefer not to discuss the human eye. Man takes the human eye for granted. For instance, when we read we are not even aware that innumerable pulses travel through the millions of optic fibers in each eye. The field of vision from each eye sends impulses to the sections of the lateral geniculate nuclei to which the optic nerves attach. These sections of the brain then send their information to columns of the visual cortex, a computer-like area in the cranium. These columns send their analysis to the appropriately related columns in the visual association cortex of the other side of the brain so that the two sides of the picture are put together again after other relays and switchings, thus making a completed visual field. Are we to say that seeing depends upon a complex teamwork of the eye and the brain is a system developed by chance? No, not hardly! Things like that do not happen by chance and the eye did not develop from "random selection." Things of that nature give indisputable evidence of a **living God**.

Theistic Evolution?

However, some will say that they believe in "theistic evolution." That has always been nonsense. I hope that our youth have not bought into it. It was put together as an accommodation to those who did not want to give up a belief in God but wanted to embrace evolution because it was **thought** to be a mark of **intelligence**. That idea has always been poppycock. God could have created the universe in any way that He saw fit but He did it the way **He said He did it!** If theistic evolution were true there would be no **Adam** and the genealogy of **Jesus** would be **false** (Luke 3: 23-38). The analogy of Jesus as the **second Adam** would also be false (Romans 5: 12-21). In fact, there are more than eight references to Adam by name in the New Testament. There are other references to his existence in such references as Matthew 19: 4. If theistic evolution were true then those wonderful words of **assurance** in I Corinthians 15: 20-22 would be **false**. The most devastating things that Christians do when they claim belief in theistic evolution is to **deny the very gospel** we preach. If there is no Adam, then there is no such thing as the **fall of man** into sin. If there is no such thing as the fall of man into sin then there is no need of redemption or a savior to save us from sin. Hence, the very gospel that we are committed to proclaim becomes a cynical mockery. Christians should **never** blaspheme the Scriptures by embracing theistic evolution or that God created the universe through evolution.

Issues of Life

There are innumerable issues related to the vital issues of life that evolution cannot answer. It cannot tell us the ultimate nature of things. It cannot reveal the ultimate origin of things. It cannot fathom past processes. It cannot predict the future. Being impersonal, it cannot control all possible forces. It cannot explain reasons why. It cannot determine what our behavior ought to be like. Dave Breese points out how helpless evolutionary science is to explain these things.

Moreover, science cannot explain such vital things that are the bedrock of such relationships as love that spouses have for one another or for their children. Evolutionary hypothesis cannot explain the emotional propositions that so influence our lives - things like compassion, joy, happiness, jealousy, envy, hatred, licentiousness, sorcery, drunkenness, or revelries. These are the things that either bring joy and happiness or snatch them away from one's life. The evolutionist cannot provide you with the spirit of love, joy, peace, long-suffering, kindness, goodness, faithfulness, gentleness, and self-control. These are the things upon which we build our lives depending upon our fellowship with God. (See Galatians 5: 19-25)

Why Is It Still With Us?

The favorite argument of the anti-God fanatics, who keep any mention of Divine Creation out of our schools, is "separation of church and state." That is a phony argument right up front. The Constitution never mentions separation of church and state. Amendment 1 says, "***Congress*** *shall make no law respecting an* *establishment of religion,* **or prohibiting the free exercise thereof,** *or breeching the freedom of speech, or the press, or the right of the people peaceably to assemble and to petition the government for a redress of grievances."* **That is the First Amendment.**

Some anti-God fanatics approached a Supreme Court Justice about this issue at one time and he said, "Congress - not the school board, not the county commissioners, not the school principal, but **Congress and Congress only**!" The first question should **always be**, "Has **Congress** made such a law?" The Constitution also guarantees the "**free exercise**" of religion. When a child is **prevented** from **praying** over his lunch, that is a violation of the First Amendment to the Constitution and a child's **right** to freely exercise his faith!. When God cannot be mentioned in the classroom, that is a violation of that child's right under the Constitution. When the creation account cannot even be referred to in class, that too is a violation of the **free exercise** clause of the **Constitution**.

Many teachers go along and teach the theory of evolution because they do not think they have any other choice. Many school boards do not allow religious activities, including the singing of Christmas carols or Easter songs. This usually happens because school boards figure that they just do not have the money to fight the fanatical organizations in the courtroom that seem to have a lot of resources these days to fight Christianity. Many parents feel that they are not qualified to confront the evolutionists. Let it be said here, that one **does not have to have a college or university degree in biology** in order to understand the bankrupt ideas of evolution. That is the reason we have shared some history about the development of evolution. Many parents deal with it by simply turning to **home schooling** where parents (usually a mother) abandon any thought of a job outside the home because they cannot entrust their children to the public school system and they do it at great sacrifice. Private academies, where parents pay expensive tuition in addition to regular school taxes, are cropping up all over the United States. Hundreds of thousands of young people are now being taught in private academies so that they can be taught the **whole** truth but many school boards do not seem to recognize their predicament or even care that the **First Amendment** rights of students are being routinely denied. Christians, is it not time for parents of students to challenge the mindless practices of evolutionists? It is our prayer that this book will give you confidence in your position that God is the creator of the heavens and the earth. The universe did not come about by chance. That is knowledge worth knowing that produces a sensible, well-balanced graduate who turns into a good citizen and community leader. Remember what Ben Stein said: "No lie can live forever."

What Others Say

"I can see how it may be possible for a man to look down upon earth and be an atheist but I cannot see how he can look up into the heavens and say there is no God."

- -- Abraham Lincoln

"If a book be false in its facts, disprove them; if false in its reasoning, refute it. But for God's sake, let us freely hear both sides if we choose."

-- Thomas Jefferson

"The visible marks of extraordinary wisdom and power appear so plainly in the works of the creation that a rational creature who will but seriously reflect on them cannot miss the discovery of a Deity."

-- John Locke

"It is impossible to account for the creation of the universe without the agency of a supreme being."

-- George Washington

"Of what I call God, and fools call nature."

-- Robert Browning

"The more I study nature, the more I stand amazed at the work of its creator."

-- Louis Pasteur

"So irresistible are these evidences of an intelligent and powerful agent that, of the infinite number of men who have excited through all the time, they have believed in the proportion a million at least to unite, in the hypothesis of an eternal pre-existence of a creator rather than in that of a self-existent universe."

-- Thomas Jefferson

Documentary Hypothesis

Third: the third thing that happened in the 19th century , **which caused unbelievable and lasting damage to the witness of Christianity,** was another **hypothesis**. It was known as the "Documentary Hypothesis." Now, the definition of a hypothesis is that it is an **assertion** that has **never been proven**. It comes from the Greek word hypotithenai (ὑποητιθέναι) which simply means, "to suppose." It is something that is stated as true for the purpose of debate, argumentation, or investigation. It is an assumption. The term **hypothetical** comes from the same root word. It refers to something that is suppositional, conjectural, conditional, or contingent. It always refers to something that is yet to be proven scientifically and it does not refer to **propositional truth**. The same is true of the term **theory**. It refers to speculation, assumption, or guess, based on limited information or knowledge and is always distinguished from **experiment or practice**. It is a form of **abstract** reasoning or **speculation**. It springs from the Greek word **theoria** (θεορια) which simply refers to a spectator or observer.

Something to Remember

The reader should always remember that when the terms hypothesis or theory are applied to a set of beliefs, it is referring to something that has not been scientifically or philosophically demonstrated to be propositional truth. The Documentary Hypothesis was advanced by **Julius Wellhausen**. The date was 1878. The work that he published was called, "Prolegomena to the History of Israel." A prolegomena is a shorter work that tells how a larger work is to be understood and interpreted. The larger work that he talked about in his prolegomena was the **Pentateuch**, or the **first five books of the Bible**, which ultimately affected the entire Bible. Since Wellhausen was a firm believer in **Darwin's theory of evolution**, he also insisted that the Old Testament was a manifestation of evolutionary thinking rather than divine revelation. To him, there was no **Adam and Eve**. These were only literary symbols. If that is true, as we pointed out earlier, the genealogy of Jesus found in the Gospel of Luke would be **false**. To Wellhausen, the Bible was no longer a book of revelation but a "crazy quilt" of folklore and human documents. He did not believe that **Moses authored the first five books of the Bible** that we refer to as the **Pentateuch**. Any discussion of divine creation must include those books because the most detailed account of creation is found in **the first of those books that we know as Genesis**. Wellhausen reached back to 1678 and the work of a Catholic Priest by the name of Richard Simon who first advanced the hypothesis that the Pentateuch had at least two authors. He thought they were, "Yahwehists" and "Elohists." Wellhausen expanded it to include Deutoronimic writers and Priestly writers. He developed the Documentary Hypothesis that was known as the JEDP theory. The theory suggested that the Pentateuch was a **compilation of documents written over a span of 5 centuries by redactors** rather than coming from the hand of **Moses**. While Wellhausen believed that Exodus was historical, he believed that everything before that was mythical.

Other Heretics

Of course, Wellhausen was not alone. Jean Astruc, who had died in 1766, was a French physician who suggested that Moses copied from two separate documents. One he called the Eloheim document and the other he called the Jehovah document. He was essentially aligned with Richard Simon, the priest. However, it was Wellhausen whose work finally linked the Pentateuch to an evolutionary process of development. To him, Moses was a mythical figure. Of course, there were also other German **rationalists** such as Albrecht Ritschl who died in 1889 and Adolph Von Harnack who died in 1930. However, who could ignore Friedrich Schleiermacher who had died in 1834. Many have referred to him as the Father of liberalism. He stressed only the ethical side of Christianity but did believe in evangelism or salvation by grace through faith. Of course, Wellhausen's brand of liberalism swept across Europe like a wildfire. It emptied the churches of Europe and finally jumped the Atlantic Ocean and came to America. In Europe, the bells were still chiming, the choirs were still singing, the candles were still being lit. As one historian described it, "The furnaces were still blowing but the fire was out." It sent a chill across the churches of Europe and England from which they have never recovered. Less than one percent of the Church Members in Europe ever attend church today. The great majestic architecture of churches and cathedrals across Europe and England are mostly silent except for the footsteps of American tourists. The story has made the rounds about a little white haired Midwestern tourist who was on a tour of Westminster Abbey. The guide was droning on and on about the things that had taken place there and the important people who had been there. The lady abruptly said, "Young man, stop your chattering. What I want to know is whether or not **anyone has been saved here lately.**"

Bushnell

An American, Horace Bushnell, who died in 1876, was considered the father of American liberalism although he never had a very great following. He rejected the doctrine of original sin and suggested that a child should never need a conversion experience because he was born good and would remain good if correctly nurtured. He rejected the Biblical warning that *"we are by **nature**, children of wrath."* (Ephesians 2:2) Paul refers to sinful and rebellious people as *"children of **disobedience**."* (Ephesians 5: 6)

The Social Gospel

Then there was the American Baptist pastor by the name of Walter Rauschenbusch who died in 1918. He pastored the Second German Baptist Church in New York City. He was concerned about some things he viewed in the community such as poor living conditions in the tenements, labor exploitation, and governmental indifference to the suffering of the poor. When he later became a professor at the Baptist Theological Seminary in Rochester, New York, he taught and wrote extensively advocating a gospel of social concerns. Some theologians refer to him as the "father of the social gospel." Wellhausen's views also gave birth to other radical theologies such as Rudolph Bultmann's demythologizing theology. He concluded that the gospel records are a collection of myths rather than a record of historical events. Bultmann adopted Martin Heidegger's philosophy of the New Testament with the outcome being a radical criticism of the New Testament text and the emerging of "form criticism" which was an attempt to discover the literary forms and sources the writers of Scriptures were using. There were also other theologians such as the, "God is dead theology" of Friedrich Nietzsche and Thomas Altizer.

There were other radical socialist theologians who sprang from Wellhausen's liberalism and we are still living with their effects today. One is the theology of "**hope**" advocated by Jurgen Moltmann. The influence of Marxism on his theology is clear. He was a great fan of the "Christian-Marxism" associated with Ernst Bloch. **Liberation theology** had its' roots in Moltmann's theology of revolution and social change. Moltmann's hope for the future was humanistic philosophy and Hegel's ideas of thesis, antithesis, and synthesis. **Thesis** was the way in which he viewed the past as chaotic. **Antithesis** is the view of the future as a kind of hope that necessitates the present work to affect change (**synthesis**).

Liberation Theology

Liberation Theology has swept across South America and almost brought the death knell to real Christian witness in part of that region. It is also prominent in Central America. Some of the leading exponents of Liberation Theology also refer to it as "Christian-Marxism." Paul Lynns contends that Liberation Theology is a "Christian coating" of Marxist socialism. Jose Porfirio Miranda compares Karl Marx to the Apostle Paul and suggests that Marxism will lead people to love one another and believes that through the Marxist "enlightenment" the idea of sin will be a thing of the past and that there is no need of salvation through Christ. There is only the need for enlightenment. In America, James Cone, of Columbia University, is the chief theoretician of Liberation Theology and, under his guidance, Liberation Theology has morphed into Black Liberation Theology. All of these radical theologies have sprung from the liberalism of Wellhausen and there seems to be no end to the radical theologies spawned by Wellhausen's heresies.

The Gospel versus Enlightenment

According to the liberal view, man did not need salvation but enlightenment. As pointed out earlier, the Bible was not considered the Word of God but was looked upon as simply a quaint little collection of documents and folklore. The German rationalism of Wellhausen eventually captured the classrooms of universities and colleges. Churches, no longer considered the Body of Christ, became little more than civic clubs. They decided that their real mission in the world was "social justice." They turned into a type of poverty program. They got involved in labor disputes. They attacked anything that resembled capitalism. Sin, as the Bible describes it, was no longer transgression of Holy God's law and His love. The only sin was failure to become involved in the group. The so-called "group think" was everywhere. Whatever philosophy captures the college and university classrooms will eventually capture the populace. Eventually, the people felt no need for the church or for redemption and they deserted in droves.

Purpose of Man

If man evolved from lower life and was not created by a **living God**, then there is no accountability to God. Sin is not a transgression of a Holy God, it is only a failure to become enlightened, or man's "stumbling upward" in the process of evolution. To them there is no **Satan** or **evil**. Shockingly enough, surveys among American Christians recently revealed that more than half of American Christians do not believe that Satan or the Holy Spirit even exist.

It is the belief of the Wellhausen liberals that God cannot be offended so, consequently, man does not need forgiveness. This would only apply to those who believe that there is a God. Of course, Marxism and Darwinism are very heavy in this kind of philosophy but both eventually produce atheists. The preachments of Karl Marx were that the demons were capitalists who built factories and opened banks that gave people jobs. His theory was that everyone must sacrifice unselfishly for the good of the community. Those duped by this philosophy are willing to do away with the "old ugly" activities of war, hatred, famine and poverty and the only salvation they want is **not** through what they consider to be the "slaughterhouse religion" of Christ's death at Calvary; but more "education" and "enlightenment". Of course, the Nazi party of Germany arose in the most "educated" and "enlightened" country on the continent at the time. Those who subscribe to this liberal thought are usually unbelievably narcissistic. They also have a distorted and convoluted idea as to what constitutes "education" and "enlightenment." In their minds, it usually means to embrace their **sick** philosophy.

American Blowback

When the Wellhausen liberalism began to make inroads into America, some brilliant American scholars strongly resisted. The primary battleground was Princeton University. It was in 1910 when faculty members there were so alarmed about the encroachment of liberalism at Princeton University that they led the General Council of the Presbyterian Church to adopt the **Five Fundamentals**. This marked the birth of what came to be known as fundamentalism. The Five Fundamentals were **the virgin birth of Jesus Christ, the infallibility of the Scriptures, the substitutionary atonement of Christ at Calvary, His bodily resurrection from the grave, and the visible return of Christ.** This movement profoundly affected Christianity in America. While the Methodists had their discipline, Southern Baptists drew up their own Baptist Faith and Message in 1925 which was much broader and spoke to more theological and church issues than the Five Fundamentals. There was, however, a tremendous movement of the fundamentalists across America. It was very strong in the northern states, even among the Baptists, because the Northern Baptist Convention had drifted much further to the left than had Baptists in the south. W.B. Riley, a highly respected Northern Baptist pastor and, at one time, president of the Northern Baptist Convention sought to turn the Northern Convention back to its' roots but many of his brethren grew weary of the struggle. Eventually, many of the mainline churches were captured by Wellhausen liberalism.

Evangelicals

Back in the late 50's and early 60's there was a movement that was termed **evangelicalism**. Some have said that the evangelicals were children of the fundamentalists. Many of them never understood the nature of the struggle. Some began to use derisive terms about the fundamentalists such as, "the fighting fundies." Many conservatives grew weary of the struggle but the liberals never grow weary and they never seem to be held accountable for their ugliness. Today, we see, even some of the evangelicals toying with compromise. They are talking about dialogue with Muslims. Some are even talking about similarities between the Muslim faith and evangelical Christianity. This movement is known as Chrislam. They place the Koran in the "saved" houses of worship. Muslims, on the other hand, are perfectly willing to kill family members who become Christians and slay Christian missionaries. Some of the so-called "mainline" denominations have suffered decline and they are merely a shadow of their former selves. Some groups in mainline churches have pulled away and formed bodies that are more conservative. Among those are the Wesleyan church, the Missouri Synod Lutheran, and the Covenant Presbyterians. Some Pentecostal groups such as the Assemblies of God have experienced phenomenal growth. While the Southern Baptist Convention has been turned back to its' historical theological roots, it remains to be seen what will happen to some other groups. The National Baptist Convention and the General Baptist Convention have remained strong. The AME Zion church has founded some colleges and seminaries and they remain strong. Of course, heresy is not a new thing in Christianity. The Apostle Paul warned the Galatians about heresy (Galatians 1: 6-8). He also warned the Corinthian church (I Corinthians 1: 10-24; II Corinthians 11: 1-15). Further, he also warned young Timothy about things that he would have to deal with eventually (I Timothy 4: 1-2; II Timothy 3: 1-5). Of course, there was Diotrophese that John warns about in his third epistle. There was a heretic in Ephesus that John would not even speak with. His name was Cerinthus. This lets us know that the struggle for fidelity to Christ and His Word is the struggle that must be won in every generation.

What Says John?

The "stack pole" of liberalism is the attack of Wellhausen on the first five books of the Bible (the Pentateuch). He contended that Moses did not write the five books. As we have mentioned earlier, he felt that there were pseudonymous writers and redactors who put together the Pentateuch. It is as though the Holy Spirit alerted John to what would eventually come and John recorded the words of Jesus about the Pentateuch. In speaking to some rebellious and unbelieving Jews after He had healed the lame man at the Pool of Bethesda, Jesus said, *"Do not think that I shall accuse you to the Father; there is one who accuses you -* **Moses**, *in whom you trust. For if you* **believed Moses**, *you would* **believe Me**; *for he* **wrote about Me**. *But if you do not believe his writings,* **how will you believe My words?**" (John 5: 45-47) Jesus made it **very clear** on this occasion that Moses was the author of the Pentateuch and He never mentioned any JEDP writers. **Jesus said Moses wrote it**. The question every believer must now ask is; "Do I believe **Jesus** or **Wellhausen**?"

John gives further warning in his second epistle when he warned "*... many deceivers have gone out into the world* **who do not confess Jesus Christ as coming in the flesh**. *This is a deceiver and an anti-Christ. Look to yourselves, that we do not lose those things which we worked for but that we may receive a full reward.* **Whoever transgresses and does not abide in the doctrine of Christ does not have God**. *He who abides in the* **doctrine of Christ has both the Father and the Son**. *If anyone comes to you and does not bring this doctrine, do not receive him into your house or greet him; for he who greets him shares in his evil deeds.*" (II John 7-11) However, does John's testimony stand alone? Not at all!

Other Testimonies

Jesus gives the account of the rich man who lifted up his voice from Hell pleading for mercy and for Lazarus to be sent to dip his finger in water and cool the rich man's parched tongue because, as the rich man said, "*I am* **tormented** *in this* **flame**." Abraham explained that there was a great gulf fixed between them and that no one could pass it. The rich man then pleaded for his five brothers that Abraham would send Lazarus back to earth to speak to his five brothers. Abraham's answer was, *"They have **Moses** and the prophets; let them hear them."* The rich man protested that if they could hear someone from the dead they would repent. Abraham's reply was, *"If they do not hear **Moses** and the prophets, neither will they be persuaded though one rise from the dead."* (Luke 16: 25 - 31)

Jesus himself invoked the name of Moses in that famous passage of John 3: 14 when he said, *"... **as Moses lifted up the serpent in the wilderness**, even so must the Son of Man be lifted up, that whosoever believes in Him should not perish but have eternal life."* Again, when Jesus was teaching in the temple at the Feast of Tabernacles, some Jews were questioning His credentials. In His reply to them He said, *"Did not **Moses give you the law**, and yet none of you keeps the law? Why do you seek to kill me?"* (John 7: 9) Jesus also mentioned Moses in the great Bread of Life discourse (John 6: 32). The fact is that Moses is mentioned numerous times in the New Testament and there is **not one reference** that expresses doubt about his existence or that he wrote the first five books of the Bible that we call the **Pentateuch**.

Therefore, the evidence is clear, if we deny the existence of Moses or that he wrote the Pentateuch, then we are denying all the writers of the New Testament and even the words of **Jesus Himself**. I am sharing these things with the reader in the hope that we will all understand how serious it is when we subscribe to pseudo-"scholarship" that denies the Mosaic authorship of the Pentateuch. It leads to other denials against the eternal Son of God who was with God in the council chambers of eternity and who came into the world, lived a sinless life, died at Calvary, and rose again from the grave, victorious over sin, death, and Hell in order to **save** the lost of all humankind for all of eternity. One who denies the Mosaic authorship of those first five books of the Bible is denying more than he can possibly understand and he trades the certainty and assurance of Jesus Christ Himself for the speculation of a 19th Century quack theologian who did not understand what he was talking about. This writer is not willing to go there.

Conclusion

In this chapter we have demonstrated beyond any shadow of doubt that God did create the heavens and the earth, and that Jesus was right there in the creation activities with the Father (John 17: 5). We can have total confidence in the teaching of the Scripture that God created the universe and that He created man from the dust of the earth breathing into him the breath of life so that he became a living soul. (Genesis 2: 7) Those who would have you embrace the teachings of Marx, Darwin or Wellhausen have little respect for the teachings of the Word of God that was totally inspired by the Holy Spirit of God. Evolution cannot tell you how or when human life began but God tells you. Why should anyone listen to the ranting of human ignorance that denies the Word of God, who has no clue as to how life began and reject the mightiest power of the universe? It is not even sensible. As for this writer, I will opt for God every time and there is no harmonizing between the Word of God and anti-God fanaticism. Yes, a thousand times over, you can believe in Divine creation. You can also trust the Bible that tells us about Divine creation, as you will see in the next chapter.

Chapter Three
Is the Bible Trustworthy?

Yes, the Bible is trustworthy because it is **propositional truth**. What is propositional truth? Propositional truth is much more than truth in which the subject is affirmed by the predicate. It is an assertion containing only logical constants and having a fixed truth-value. The word for truth as used in such passages as John 14: 6 is **alethia** (αληθεϊα). It is not only a reference to **ethical** truth but it is also fullness of the truth in all its scope, as well as fullness of reality as embodied in Christ. Biblical truth will always stand the test of the most competent analysis or examination except for those who purpose in their hearts to deceive. Propositional truth will always be truth under any and all circumstances. This is important to remember because there are so many voices among us who want to put forth some personal twist about the truth of Scripture and say, "That is what it means to me." The truth is, however, that the Scripture is the same for everybody. What is true for one is true for everyone. There is not one truth that is applicable to one person and something different or even opposing truth that is applicable to another person. Propositional truth can never be personalized because it is God's truth. If it is wrong for one person to lie, it is wrong for everyone to lie. If it is wrong for one person to steal, it is wrong for everyone to steal. That is what propositional truth is all about. That is Biblical truth. **Biblical truth is absolute**. Biblical truth withstands all philosophical examinations. For instance, it withstands the **correspondence** examination. This simply means that truth corresponds to all known and relevant facts, not theories or hypotheses - but **facts**. Biblical truth conforms to **reality**. In other words, it **identifies things as they are**.

Propositional Biblical truth is **coherent** with all relevant and truthful data. This means that Biblical truth is **never** self-contradictory. There are times when some humans have thought that they have found contradictions in the Bible but that is because the human mind is finite and God is infinite. Propositional truth is also truth that is also **pragmatic** because it is **workable** (see Isaiah 1: 18-26).

Revelational

God's truth is also revelational. God has revealed Himself to man. That revelation has come through the Bible. Thus, the revelation is set in history and we learn about God as we read about His dealings with man through history. Christians contend that the Bible is true because it would make no sense for God to reveal Himself through wrongly recorded history. Our God is the ultimate in reason. It was not idle talk when the Prophet Isaiah recorded the inspired words of God which say, *"Come let us reason together saith the Lord."* (Isaiah 1: 18) Israel had become calloused and perfunctory in their worship of God and their religious activities had no effect on the sinful way in which they were living. God was saying to them that they were living lives that were not even reasonable and that they would live a life of blessing if they lived in obedience to the commands of God, which **were** reasonable.

An Inerrant Word

God also set the revelation of Himself in the universe. That is the heart of the cosmological evidence for the existence of God. What, therefore, the Bible tells us about the universe is true. The heavens do really *"declare the glory of God."* (Psalm 19: 1) What sense would it make for God to give His revelation in a book that was **wrong** concerning the **universe**? Because the scriptures of the Old and New Testaments are God's words by which He reveals Himself to man, the vast majority of Christians believe that the Bible is inerrant in its content and infallible in its pronouncements. It is because of the fact that what the Scriptures say is what God says. This does not mean that there cannot be scientific or philosophical studies. There is still much that man needs to learn about God's universe but he will never learn anything that is propositionally true which is in contradiction to the Holy Scriptures. This is not to say that man should not continue to do scientific research. While God has spoken to us **truthfully** in the Scriptures, that does not mean that He has spoken to us **exhaustively**. Let us never forget that God is infinite and man is finite. There is still much for us to learn about our universe and God's creation. For instance, many of the miracle drugs that have brought cures for terrible diseases are extracted from things that God has provided in our world and new cures are discovered regularly to cure diseases from compounds extracted from God's creation.

Moreover, the Holy Scriptures are given to us by inspiration of the Holy Spirit. Since Jesus is the personification of **truth**, then the Holy Spirit guides us to Jesus because the Scriptures declare that, *"He will guide you into all truth."* (John 14: 6; 16:13)

Propositional Truth

We are contending that Biblical truth is **propositional truth**, which is absolute because it is **unchanging**. It means that what the Bible says is true regardless of who does or does not believe it. For instance, there was a time when a number of people were just sure that the earth was flat. They **thought** they got that message from the Bible but **they did not**. It came from **human reasoning**. I once knew a man who thought the earth was flat. He

101

was living in a section of Oklahoma that appeared to be as flat as a floor. He believed that in spite of the fact that seamen had proved years ago that the earth was round. Finally, when men were able to put up satellites, they revealed, that indeed, the earth was round. They then understood that Isaiah was correct when he described God as *"He who sits above the **circle** of the earth ..."* No, that does not refer to any uninformed theory about a pagan belief in a "canopy." It simply refers to what is really true. The **earth is circular** (Isaiah 40:22). The man was a good man morally but he was very emphatic about his belief that the earth was flat. Sometimes, it was probably easier to agree with him than to debate him because he thought the only reality was what he could see with the naked eye but his eyes could not deliver to his brain the ultimate reality that the Word of God delivers. He was not necessarily an unintelligent person. He had skills and could do many things that others could not do. His problem was that his standard of reality was based upon what his eyes could see. His favorite by-word was, "Seeing is believing." However, that is not always true. In the part of the country where he lived, there were times, on a hot day, when a person who was not familiar with the territory would just declare that he saw a lake of water out there in front but really there was no lake there. It was a mirage.

Biblical truth is always true no matter what the circumstances appear to be. It is true, even if one cannot understand what he reads. When Jesus was brought before Pilate, He was asked of Pilate if He was a King. In Jesus' reply He stated why He had come into the world when He said, *"... that I should bear witness to the **truth**. **Every**one who is of the **truth** hears My voice."* (John 18: 37) When Pilate heard this, his question was, *"What is truth?"* He did not wait for an answer but went back out to the Jews and said, *"**I find no fault in Him**."* (John 18: 38) There was, however, something about Jesus that got through to Pilate. It is hard to escape the conclusion that, deep in Pilate's heart, he knew that

Jesus was truth and that he was **looking truth in the face**. Finally, he felt a need to do something that would absolve him of responsibility for what was taking place so he went through that childish process of washing his hands.

What Saith John?

John speaks of **truth** more than any other Gospel writer does. In the first chapter of his Gospel he describes the incarnation of Jesus when he said, *"The **Word** became **flesh** and dwelt **among us**, and we beheld His glory, the glory as of the only begotten of the Father, full of grace and **truth**."* (John 1: 14) Thus, in the very beginning of his Gospel, John makes it clear that Jesus is the very **personification** of truth. He amplifies it in verse 17 of that same chapter when he points out that *"The law was given through Moses, but grace and **truth** came through Jesus Christ."* He closes out his marvelous prologue by pointing out that while *"No one has seen God at any time, the **only begotten Son**, who is in the bosom of the Father, **He has declared Him**."* (John 1: 18) Therein, do we have the purpose of Jesus coming into the world that was to declare the whole **truth** of God as well as to *"**seek and save** that which was **lost**."* (Luke 19: 9)

Did Jesus support John's contention? Absolutely! It was only hours before Jesus would be crucified when Phillip asked those piercing words: *"Lord, show us the Father, and it is sufficient for us."* Jesus' reply was, *"Have I been with you so long, and yet you have not known Me, Phillip? He who has seen **Me** has seen the **Father**, so how can you say, '**Show us the Father**'?"* However, Phillip was not the only one who was slow to understand. Just before Phillip asked his question, Thomas had asked him, *"Lord, we do not know where You are going, how can we know the way?"* As pointed out earlier Jesus said to him, *"I am the way, the **truth**,* and the life. No one comes to the Father except through me." (John 14: 5-6)

A Part of the Godhead

John makes clear, not only who Jesus was and why he came but that He was part of the Godhead when He said, "*I am in the Father and the Father in Me.*" In that very verse He gave us a world of reason to believe everything that He said and taught when He said, "**Believe Me** *that I am in the* **Father** *and the Father in* **Me**, *or else* **believe Me for the sake of the works themselves.**" (John 14: 11) He also declared that belief in Him brings empowerment to our lives when He said, "*Most assuredly, I say to you, he who* **believes in Me**, *the works that I do will he do also; and greater works than these he will do because I go to My Father.*" (John 14: 12) Not only does He empower but also He asserts that if we love **Him**, we are to keep His commandments (John 14: 15). It is on that basis that He will do whatever we ask in His name that **will glorify the Father** (John 14: 13). That is an instructive verse because it lets us know we should not ask anything in Jesus' name **unless it will glorify the Father**. All of that is a part of what it means when Jesus declares that He is the **personification of truth**.

Truth is a very large theme in the Gospel of John. To John, truth was indisputable. Truth was truth under all circumstances. Truth was truth whether or not men believed it. To John, it was never "almost truth" but it was truth that was pure and unadulterated. There was no compromise. To him, truth always rose above the standards of the world. Truth always had to rise to the level of the character of Jesus. **John lived** in a world in which there were some who wanted to say a few good things about Jesus but then they would mix in something that was not truth. John would have none of it. Spurgeon once warned that the struggle was not always between **truth** and **falsehood** but often the struggle was between **truth** and **almost truth**. He shared John's views.

In John's world, truth was **never relative**. With man, truth can sometimes be relative. For instance, if I say that I like vegetable soup, that may be truth for me but someone else may not like vegetable soup. That kind of truth is relative to the taste of the individual but with **God's truth**, there is **never** any relativity. Truth is truth for everyone when we come to the Word of God.

Relative Truth

Too many times, we have known of Christians getting into **relative truth** that is never **God's truth**. The person who is dabbling in relative truth likes to pick and choose what parts of the Bible he will accept and what parts he will reject. Man will often conclude that, "This is what **works for me**." For instance, this writer heard a well-known religious leader who was repulsed at the idea that Jesus was the **only way of salvation** in spite of the fact that Jesus assured His followers that He was "*the way, the truth and the life.*" He further stated that no one could come to the Father except through Him. No man has the right to say that Jesus is simply "**a way**"; He is "**the way**." Who cannot get you to the Father? Mohammed cannot get you to the Father. Maharishi cannot get you to the Father. Hari Krishna cannot get you to the Father. Buddha cannot get you to the Father. It is only Jesus, God's Son, who can get you to the Father.

Companion of Grace

As John drew near to the end of his prologue, he points out that **grace** is a companion of **truth** and that the **grace** of God was to be a continually **growing** and expanding thing in our lives. Christ was full of grace. He asserts that there was some grace given under the Law of Moses but **grace and truth** came by Jesus Christ (John 1: 16-17). Moreover, the Bible often compares the Gospel message to **light**. For instance, John points out that *"In Him was life and the life was the light of men. And the light shineth in darkness and the darkness comprehended it not."* (John 1: 4-5) Jesus taught Nicodemus that condemnation came into the world because the world loved **darkness** rather than **light** and they loved that **darkness** because their **deeds were evil**. He was careful to make Nicodemus understand that those who **do evil hate the light** and will not come to the light unless their deeds should be **reproved**. Who then comes to the light? Jesus said it well: *"He that doeth **truth** cometh to the **light**, that his deeds may be made manifest, that they are wrought in God."* (John 3: 19-21)

Jacob's Well

When Jesus dealt with the woman at the well, He revealed to her that real worship of the Father must come by **truth**. The woman was confused about what He meant concerning the water that Jesus would give her that would quench her spiritual thirst forever. His message to her was that, *"Whoever drinks of this **water that I shall give him** will never thirst. But the water that I shall give him will become in him a **fountain of water** springing up into everlasting life."* (John 4: 14) The woman was also confused about where they could worship, whether they should worship at the mountain near Sychar or in Jerusalem. Jesus stated to her that it was neither but that, *"The hour is coming when you will neither on this mountain nor in Jerusalem worship the Father. ....but the hour is coming, and now is, when the **true** worshippers will worship the Father in **spirit** and in **truth** for the Father is seeking such to worship Him."* (John 4: 21-24) In fact, Jesus declared to her that

*"God is a **spirit** and those who worship Him **must worship Him in Spirit and in truth.**"* (John 4: 24)

Truth and Freedom

Jesus authenticated his Word when He said, *"He who sent me is **true**; and I speak to the world those things which I heard from **Him**."* (John 8: 26) Jesus assured them that when He was *"**lifted up**"* then they would know that He was from the Father. This, of course, refers to His crucifixion and the things that surrounded His crucifixion such as darkness falling over the earth at noonday, the rending of the veil of the temple, the quaking of the earth, and the opening of the graves. Even the Centurion cried out, *"**Truly, this man was the Son of God.**"* Jesus assured them that in that hour the Father would be with Him.

Jesus declared to the Jews who believed in Him in order to give them assurance. He said to them, *"If you abide in my word, you are my disciples indeed and you shall know the **truth, and the truth shall make you free.**"* (John 8: 31-32) Again, we find that **truth** is **inexorably** linked to our **freedom in Christ**. We learn here that the Scriptures are all about conveying God's truth to us and it is **that truth** that leads us to salvation. That truth **strengthens us** in living the Christian life. That truth brings to us the light of the Gospel. It is that **truth** that makes us **free** and it is that **truth** that will ultimately **take us to God's presence!**

Right and Wrong

Therefore, we have learned that **right** and **wrong** is not a decision or a choice that the individual makes in an arbitrary manner but it is something that we **discover**. For instance, we often hear people say, "I have been taught to think for myself and decide for myself what is right and wrong." That is always disastrous and it is illogical. For instance, someone may decide that they are **justified** in **killing** another person. They think that someone, in their mind, has wronged them and they have a right to take a life. Others think that it is fine to kill a **baby** while it is in the womb. That has been advanced in our time to include a baby as it is leaving the womb at the time of delivery. It is called "partial birth abortion." The world calls it, "a woman's right to choose" and it quite ignores the Biblical teaching concerning the sacredness of human life. Others have decided that it is quite all right to ignore the Biblical prohibition concerning adultery. They decide that prostitution is all right but then they learn that immorality extracts a terrible price from the offender when their bodies are wracked with incurable diseases and such diseases can diminish their bodies and even their mind.

This writer knew of a Christian man who had lived an exemplary life. After retirement, he was caught up in an immoral act that lead to other transgressions of the law - not only of **man** but also of **God**. When the police were arresting him he said, "It's not wrong because it is in the Bible. It's in the Bible because it is wrong." He had recognized that the Bible's prohibition against what he had done was for the good of him and all mankind and that to violate that prohibition brought great harm to him, his family, and everyone that he knew. That is the reason Christians always insist that the commands of God are for our good and our **own happiness**. That was the lesson that even Adam and Eve had to learn the hard way in the Garden of Eden. It was not the act of eating the forbidden fruit but it was the act of disobedience and the condition of their mind and heart that led them to disobey God.

Sophism

Sometimes **sin against God** is described as "open mindedness" or "adapting to the times." The notion that each person decides for himself or herself what is his or her own truth is not a thing in the world but a return to ancient pre-Socratic sophism or paganism. The Bible warns of those who try to live by their own rules. In Moses' third oration when he was giving the law of the central sanctuary, he declared to the people that *"You shall not at all do as we are doing here today - every man doing whatever is right **in his own eyes** --."* (Deuteronomy 12: 8) Tragically, many are living that way at the present time! The identical warnings appear twice in the lawless days of the judges (Judges 17:6; 21: 25). This is the reason that pagan customs such as child murder or infanticide, adultery, fornication and other filthy disease causing and life wrecking sins are becoming more and more **acceptable**. The so-called "woman's right to choose" is not one iota more civilized than the boorish and pagan practice by ancient Romans of simply throwing a new born child on the trash heap if its' appearance didn't please the father or if the sex of the baby was not what he preferred. That is the reason Christianity must trumpet the **propositional truths** of the Word of God articulated in the Bible as *"a light that shines in a dark place, until the day dawns and the morning star rises in your hearts; knowing this first, that no prophecy of Scripture is of any **private interpretation**, for prophecy never came by the will of man, but **holy men of God** spoke as they were **moved** by the **Holy Spirit**."* (II Peter 1: 19-21)

The Bible Is Inerrant

What then, can we say about the **nature** of Scripture? What does John have to say about the **inerrancy** of Scripture? One of the very profound statements that Jesus made, as quoted by John, was that *"You search the **Scriptures**, for in them you think you have eternal life; and these are they which **testify of me**."* When Jesus announces the coming of the Holy Spirit and that He would take over the administration of the Kingdom of God in the world he said: *"However, when he, the spirit of **truth**, has come, he will guide you into **all truth**, for whatever he hears he will speak; and he will tell you things to come. He will glorify me, for he will take of what is mine and declare it to you. All things that the Father has are mine. Therefore I said that he will take of mine and declare it unto you."* (John 16: 13-15) The phrase that jumps out at us there is that declaration of Jesus Himself who said, *"He will **guide you into all truth**."* He is speaking to several men who would be **writers** of the **New Testament**. We have talked about Biblical truth and how it is propositional, absolute, and unchanging. It is the words of Jesus Himself that the Holy Spirit would so inspire them that they would be guided into **"all"** truth. The word "all," translated from the Greek word "pasan" (πασαν), is an intensive, which means whole, complete or entire. It is a declaration that **every single part of the whole** is included. Jesus adds a decisive factor in His great intercessory prayer before His crucifixion. When He was praying for His disciples, He said, *"Sanctify them by your **truth**. **Your word is truth**."* (John 17:17) These are the words He spake just before He was arrested. The sum of it is that the Bible gives us all the truth we need to be right with God and have eternal life through Jesus Christ. It is the **truth** of Scripture that strengthens us and separates us unto **His** service.

Jesus Was a Part of the Godhead

Some agnostics and infidels will argue that the New Testament had not been written yet when Jesus spoke these words but, indeed, the New Testament is a record of what Jesus did and taught. He is a part of the Godhead who was there with God in the very beginning. Let us **never forget that.** He knew not only what would be written in the New Testament but He knew how the world would receive it and He made that clear in His prayer. Yes, these are the inspired words of John but they correspond to the other teachings of the Word of God concerning the inerrancy of Scripture. This is confirmed by the pronouncement of Jesus in the Sermon on the Mount when He said, *"Do not think that I came to destroy the law or the prophets. I did not come to destroy but to **fulfill**. For assuredly, I say to you, till heaven and earth pass away, one **jot** or **one tittle** will by no means pass from the law till all is **fulfilled**."* (Matthew 5: 17-18) The Sermon on the Mount was one of the most important messages that Jesus delivered while on this earth. One might call it the "Christian Manifesto" because much of what He taught during the remainder of His ministry was first set forth in the Sermon on the Mount.

These same mighty truths were set forth by Paul when he said, *"For whatever things were written before were written for our learning, that we through the patience and comfort of the **scriptures** might have **hope**."* (Romans 15: 4) Paul underscores the same powerful truth as he writes to Timothy when he said, *"... from childhood you have known the holy scriptures, which are **able to make you wise for salvation through faith which is in Christ Jesus. All scripture** is given by **inspiration of God**, and is profitable for doctrine, for reproof, for correction, for instruction in righteousness."* (II Timothy 3: 15-16) Instructions in **doctrine** refer to the things that we must believe from the Word of God. The term "**reproof**" refers to the things we should reject. "**Correction**" is the pointing out of false teaching we should avoid. "**Instruction in righteousness**" refers to the correct teaching from the Word of God for Godly living.

The writer of Hebrews drives home the same great truth. In the opening verses of the first chapter when he said, *"God, who at various times and in different ways spoke in time past to the fathers by the prophets, has in these last days spoken to us by* **His Son,** *whom He has appointed heir of all things, through whom also* **He made the worlds;** *who being in the brightness of His glory and the express image of His person, and upholding all things by the word of His power, when He had by Himself purged our sins, set down at the right hand of the majesty on high, having become so much better than the angels, as He has by inheritance obtained a more excellent name than they."* (Hebrews 1: 1-4) Moreover, it was Peter who quoted from the powerful 40th chapter of Isaiah when he said, *"The word of the Lord endures* **forever.***"* (I Peter 1: 25)

What Inerrancy Does Not Mean

The inerrancy of Scripture does not mean that there cannot be different styles of writing in the Bible. When Jesus declared to the disciples that the Holy Spirit would "guide" them into all truth, He did not even hint that the Holy Spirit would "dictate" to them. He would **guide** them in such a way that what they wrote would be absolute **truth**! The Bible was written over a period of hundreds of years. Of course, David's Psalms do not have the same style as the writing of Luke or John. When we say that the Holy Spirit has "**guided**" the Biblical authors we are saying that those authors were so **guided** by the Holy Spirit that what they wrote **was** the complete and absolute truth of God and that there were **no errors** in their work. The fact that the Holy Spirit allowed each author to write in his own style gives us wonderful variety in the Scripture as well as poetic beauty. For instance, the writings of Isaiah have a soaring pathos about them while the writings of David have a poetic meter about them.

Passage Through Jericho

Moreover, inerrancy does not mean that the writers described the same incident in exactly the same way. For instance, as Jesus was **coming into** Jericho before He met Zacchaeus, the Scriptures tell us that a blind man met Him and Jesus healed his sight because of his faith (Luke 19: 42-43). It was Jesus' last trip through Jericho before His crucifixion. He would leave Jericho and go on up to Jerusalem for the Passover where He was crucified. When Matthew records that passage through Jericho, he does not tell of Jesus dining with Zacchaeus as Luke does, rather Matthew tells of His charge to the disciples and the approach of James and John's Mother, the wife of Zebedee. Matthew also records the healing of two blind men as Jesus was **departing** Jericho. (Matthew 20: 29-33) Does that mean that one of the Gospel writers was wrong? Not at all. They simply recorded different events about the same journey through Jericho. When we compare the two writers, we see that Luke described the healing of a blind man on the way **into** Jericho and Matthew described the healing of **two** blind men as Jesus **left** the city of Jericho.

All three of the synoptic Gospels (Matthew, Mark, and Luke) record the ministry of Jesus in a type of chronological order. They do not always say the same thing about the same events but they do not **contradict** one another. That is the reason they **complement** one another. We are all aware that two people can view an automobile accident. They can both describe it **accurately** but they will not say exactly the same thing about it. That is the beauty of the Spirit allowing Biblical writers to tell the **truth** in their own words.

Estimations and Approximations

Neither does Biblical inerrancy demand exact numbers nor does it prohibit estimations or approximations. For instance, when Luke records the happenings on the day of Pentecost in the book of Acts, he says there were *"**about** 3,000 souls"* who were saved. He did not take a head count but he made an approximation and with the **Holy Spirit's guidance**, that approximation was true. As we pointed out earlier, 92% of the Gospel of John is not found in the other Gospels. However, as we compare all four of the Gospels to one another we have a beautiful, moving, and well-rounded account of the ministry of Jesus on earth that is true. However, John closes out his Gospel by pointing out that *"There are also many other things that Jesus did, which if they were written one by one, I suppose that even the **world itself could not contain the books that would be written.**"* (John 21: 25)

Beware of Heretics

Heretics, who believe that the Bible is full of ancient, culturally affected documents and folklore will often ask the childish and shallow question as to "What version of the Bible is inerrant? Is it the King James, the NIV, American Standard Version, or the New English Version?" That should never dismay the earnest Christian who believes the Bible because we understand that it does not matter what version of the Bible or into what language it is translated. If it is translated properly and it is true to the original languages, then it is inerrant. So, a Bible properly translated, whether it be into Latin, German, Japanese or any other hundreds of dialects, it is still inerrant if the translation has been true to the original languages as have been confirmed by extant manuscripts. The original autographs of the Bible were written in Hebrew, a limited amount of Aramaic, and Greek. That is the reason that

114

Biblical scholars make careful studies of the Biblical and cognate languages before attempting to make a translation. The Bible has been translated into hundreds of dialects but it is always inerrant as long as it is true to the most ancient extant manuscripts. That is what inerrancy is all about. It means that the **propositional** truth of God as given to the divinely inspired Biblical writers is correctly recorded and without error. That means, that when all the facts and historical background is correctly known, the Scriptures, in their original autographs and properly understood will be found completely and absolutely true in everything they teach. If they speak on a scientific subject then the Biblical account will be true. If they speak concerning doctrine, the Biblical account is true. If they speak concerning history, geography, geology, or any other discipline, the Bible will always be true and can be trusted. Even though the Biblical account may not be exhaustive in some disciplines, it will **always be true** in what it teaches! This has been repeatedly proven and the believer who embraces the truth of the Word of God will live a happy, exemplary, and Godly life.

To suggest that God's Word contains errors is to impugn the very nature and character of God. To suggest that the Bible contains errors is to suggest that God failed in His effort to communicate with his creation.

Cynics

Some cynical liberals have insisted that we can learn proper Christian lessons even from a Bible that contains errors. Of course, that is nothing more than a lot of irrational blather or nonsense. Such people are never able to give a definitive criterion for determining which supposed errors are immaterial to them or who decides the boundaries between what "permissible" inerrancy is and what is not.

When the inerrancy of Scripture is properly understood, it means that the Bible speaks with authority and is **accurate** in all of its assertions whether those assertions are theological, historical, geographical, scientific, geological, or creational. Inerrancy does not demand rigidity of style. In all Biblical statements there is to be found accuracy in accordance with the truth of God, which, again, is **propositional truth**! Because the Bible is Divinely inspired by a loving God, and is *"God breathed"* by a God **who does not *"breathe error"*** it is a beautiful panorama of holy truth that inspires us, guides us, rebukes our waywardness, shows us the way of salvation and comforts us in our time of need. Yes, the Bible is totally trustworthy!

Messianic Prophecies

The most moving and accurate internal testimony concerning the inerrancy of Scripture is the prophecies of the Scripture concerning the coming of Jesus, the Messiah, that is prophesied in the Old Testament and fulfilled in the New Testament. Some of them are as follows:

Old Testament	Announcement of Prophecy	New Testament Fulfillment
Micah 5:2 *"But thou Bethlehem Ephratah, though thou be little among the thousands of Judah, yet out of thee shall he come forth unto me that is to be ruler in Israel; whose goings forth unto me that is to be ruler in Israel; whose goings forth have been from of old, from everlasting."*	Born in Bethlehem	Luke: 2: 4, 5 & 7 *"And Joseph also went up from Galilee, out of the city of Nazareth, into Judea, unto the city of David, which is called Bethlehem; because he was of the house and lineage of David:) To be taxed with Mary his espoused wife, being great with child. And she brought forth; her first-born son, and wrapped him in swaddling clothes, and laid him in a manger; because there was no room for them in the inn."*

Old Testament	Announcement of Prophecy	New Testament Fulfillment
"Isaiah 7: 14 *"Therefore the Lord himself shall give you a sign; Behold a virgin shall conceive, and bear a son, and shall call his name Immanuel."*	Born of a virgin	Luke 1: 26,27, 30, 31 *"And in the sixth month the angel Gabriel was sent from God unto a city of Galilee, named Nazareth,* *To a virgin espoused to a man whose name was Joseph, of the house of David, and the virgin's name was Mary,* *And the angel said unto her, Fear not Mary; for thou hast found favor with God.* *And, behold, thou shalt conceive in thy womb, and bring forth a son, and shalt call his name Jesus."*

Old Testament	Announcement of Prophecy	New Testament Fulfillment
Isaiah 61: 1-2 *"The spirit of the Lord God is upon me; because the Lord hath anointed me to preach good tidings unto the meek; he hath sent me to bind up the brokenhearted, to proclaim liberty to the captives, and the opening of the prison to them that are bound:* *To proclaim the acceptable year of the Lord and the day of vengeance of our God; to comfort all that mourn."*	To heal the broken hearted	Luke 4: 18-19 *"The Spirit of the Lord is upon me, because he hath anointed me to preach the gospel to the poor; he hath sent me to heal the broken hearted, to preach deliverance to the captives and recovering of sight to the blind, to set at liberty them that are bruised.* *To preach the acceptable year of the Lord."*

Old Testament	Announcement of Prophecy	New Testament Fulfillment
Isaiah 61: 1-2 *"He is despised and rejected of men, a man of sorrows, and acquainted with grief; and we hid as it were our faces from him; he was despised and we esteemed him not."*	Rejected by His own people	John 1: 11 *"He came unto His own, and His own received Him not."*
Psalm 35: 19 *"Let not them that are mine enemies wrongfully rejoice over me; neither let them wink with the eye that hates me without a cause."*	Despised without a cause	John 15: 24-25 *"If I had not done among them the works which none other man did, they had not had sin; but now have they both seen and hated both me and my Father. But this cometh to pass, that the word might be fulfilled that is written in their law, They hated me without a cause."*

Old Testament	Announcement of Prophecy	New Testament Fulfillment
Zechariah 12: 10 *"And I will pour upon the house of David, and upon the inhabitants of Jerusalem, the spirit of grace and of supplications; and they shall look upon me whom they have pierced, and they shall mourn for him, as one mourneth for his only son, and shall be in bitterness for him, as one that is in bitterness for his first-born."*	Pierced through His hands and feet	John 20: 27 *"Then saith he to Thomas, 'Reach hither thy finger, and behold my hands; and reach hither thy hand, and thrust it into my side; and be not faithless, but believing.'"*

Old Testament	Announcement of Prophecy	New Testament Fulfillment
Psalm 34: 20 *"He keepeth all his bones; not one of them is broken."*	Not a bone broken	John 19: 32, 33, 36 *"Then came the soldiers, and brake the legs of the first, and of the other which was crucified with him."* *"But when they came to Jesus and saw that he was dead already, they brake not his legs:"* *"For these things were done, that the scripture should be fulfilled, A bone of him shall not be broken."*
Psalm 16: 10 *"For thou wilt not leave my soul in hell; neither wilt thou suffer thine Holy One to see corruption."*	Raised from the dead	Mark 16: 6-7 *"And he saith unto them, Be not affrighted; Ye seek Jesus of Nazareth, which was crucified; he is risen; he is not here; behold the place where they laid him. But go your way, tell his disciples and Peter that he goeth before you into Galilee; there*

		shall ye see him, as he said unto you."

Old Testament	Announcement of Prophecy	New Testament Fulfillment
Psalm 68:18 *"Thou hast ascended on high, thou hast led captivity captive; thou hast received gifts for men; yes, for the rebellious also, that the Lord God might dwell among them."*	Our Lord's ascension	Mark 16: 19 *"So then after the Lord had spoken unto them, he was received up into them, he was received up into heaven, and sat on the right hand of God."* *I Corinthians 15: 4* *"And that he was buried, and that he rose again the third day according to the scriptures:"* *Ephesians 4: 8* *"Wherefore he saith, When he ascended up on high, he led captivity captive, and gave gifts unto men."*

Conclusion

The truth of the Bible rests upon facts! For instance, the greatest event of the Old Testament, aside from Creation, was the exodus of the Children of Israel from Egypt. Liberal scholars have long attempted to disprove the Biblical account of the crossing at the Red Sea. Harper's Bible Dictionary points out that there are two or three different routes that have been proposed as to the path of the Israelites after leaving Egypt. We have to remember that the crossing of the Red Sea came **after** the Israelites had left Egypt. It was Major Jarvis who pointed out that Israel probably never visited what is now known as Jebel Musā (Mount Moses) which was declared sacred as late as the fourth century AD. Liberal theologians declared that they crossed an area known as the "Reed Sea" which was a marshy land just north of the Suez Gulf. Of course, anyone who understands anything of logistics would know that moving approximately two million people with carts, draft animals, and cattle through marshland would create deadly bogs that would be impassible. Only the naïve have ever embraced that idea. It is to be remembered that God lead the Children of Israel by a pillar of cloud by day and a pillar of fire by night. We remember the childhood song that we used to sing in Church that said, "God knows the way through the wilderness. All we have to do is follow." Through God's leadership, He kept the Israelites near sources of water and grazing land. The pillar of cloud by day and the pillar of fire by night indicate that they moved in haste, perhaps fearing pursuit by the Egyptian Army. They travelled day and night for a time.

Gulf of Aqaba

It is known that they travelled to the Gulf of Aqaba. The Jordan rift continues below the Dead Sea to the northern end of the Gulf of Aqaba and on the west side of the Gulf is a large beach area known as Nuweiba. From 1978 until 1987 Archaeologist Ron Wyatt discovered by a process of sounding a land bridge that runs across the Gulf of Aqaba that is only about 200 feet deep at its' lowest point but it provides a land bridge across the Gulf of Aqaba that slopes gently down to 200 feet and back up to the other side where there is another beach on the Arabian side. On either side of that land bridge, the Gulf of Aqaba is very deep; as deep as a mile in some places. Even with the water gone the slopes would be so steep that it would be very difficult or impossible for animals to go down one side and up the other but the land bridge provided a gentle slope that the people could cross over safely. **On that land bridge divers have found wheels of chariots, skeletons of horses, chariot bodies and human skeletons indicating, indeed, that Pharaoh's Army drowned in that part of the Red Sea.** Some of the chariot wheels are encrusted with coral but some of them were overlaid with gold and had gold hubs. Coral will not grow on gold.

Indisputable Evidence

Underwater photographers have made pictures of the chariot wheels as they lay because the wooden parts are so deteriorated it would be difficult to move them. The pictures indicate that the chariot wheels found on the bottom of the Red Sea are identical to the wheels that were found in the Tomb of Tutankhamen in 1978. A first column that was erected by Solomon partially submerged in water to mark the place of the Israelite crossing. A second column was found in 1984 which still contained some of the inscriptions such as Mizraim (Egypt), Solomon; Edom; Death; Pharaoh; Moses; and Yahweh (Jehovah). King Solomon had set up the columns as a memorial to the miracle of the Red Sea crossing. It has now been confirmed that the Children of Israel did cross the

Red Sea **exactly as it was recorded in the Scriptures** and there is abundant evidence to support the Biblical record. We see again that, when we find archaeological evidence of the period, it always supports the Scriptures that we have. **Yes, we can trust the Scriptures!** However, multiplied millions of Christians would still believe the Scriptures whether the evidence had been found or not because they know that God has passed down the Scriptures through the ages, miraculously intact, so that men of every age may have a source of revealed truth by which to live. **The Bible is divinely inspired and is without error!**

Chapter Four
Is the Church Important?

Yes, because Jesus loved the church and **gave himself for it**. (Ephesians 5: 27) The Church of our Lord faces critical days. The church is even being attacked and sometimes persecuted right here in our own country that was founded upon the basis of religious freedom. This is nothing new. Throughout history, the church has been attacked and persecuted. Even the first church that was formed in Jerusalem on the day of Pentecost was so persecuted that the members had to pool their resources just to exist and the Apostle Paul, on his missionary journeys raised money for the saints in Jerusalem.

Sometimes, the church has fallen into the hands of charlatans who would shed the blood of others in the name of the church. Some of the bloodiest times in history are those of the Spanish Inquisition. Terrible things were done in the name of the church in the city of Geneva, Switzerland during the days of John Calvin's magisterial religious rule. The Pilgrims fled to America because of their treatment at the hand of King James. For many years, the church in America has enjoyed freedom of worship, but that is now changing. Churches are being denied building permits in some places. The free exercise of religion is being denied even though the First Amendment to the Constitution guarantees it.

It is sad, however, to hear people say, "I don't need the church." Some are saying, "I can be a Christian without the church." It is disturbing to see what some charlatans are now doing in the name of the church, but still the church marches on!

John's Example

John did not theorize about the church. What he taught about the church he taught by example. What he wrote about the church is mostly found in the book of the Revelation, which we will discuss at length. How can we measure John's attitude toward the church?John, along with the other disciples was present with Jesus at Caesarea Philippi when Peter confessed that Jesus was *"the Christ, the son of the living God."* It was then that Jesus promised the founding of the church. When Peter made that great confession that Jesus was the Christ of God, Jesus told him that he had received that revelation from the Father in Heaven. At that point Jesus said, *"Thou art Peter, and upon this rock I will build my church; and the gates of Hell shall not prevail against it."* (Matthew 16: 18, KJV) When Jesus said, *"Thou art Peter,"* the Greek word was *"petros"* (πετρος). It is masculine and refers to a **small stone** or pebble that can be thrown. However, when Jesus referred to the building of the **church** He used the word *"petra"* (πετρα). That word is feminine and refers to **bedrock** that is immovable and refers back to **Jesus Himself**. The idea is that Peter understands who Jesus really is and that confession has made him a part of Jesus, **the bedrock**. The same root word was used when Jesus concluded the **Sermon on the Mount**. He said, *"Whoever **hears these sayings of mine** and does them, I will liken him unto a wise man, who **built his house upon the rock.**"* The word is *"petran"* (πετραν). (Matthew 7:24-25) This is the same gender as the word used by Jesus in speaking of building His church in Matthew 16 at Caesarea, Philippi. What is He saying? He is saying, "The person who will build his life upon **Me** and the **teachings** that I have given you here today will be like a man who built his house on a rock who can withstand the **storms of life.** But, the person who builds his life upon the **shifting sands of the world** will collapse when the **storms come**." Edward Mote caught the message well back in 1832:

"My hope is built on nothing less
Than Jesus' blood and righteousness;
I dare not trust the sweetest frame,
But, wholly lean on Jesus' name.
When darkness seems to hide his face,
I rest on his unchanging grace,
In every high and stormy gale,
My anchor holds within the veil.
On Christ, the **solid Rock**, I stand;
All other ground is sinking sand,
All other ground is sinking sand."

What Means the Rock?

Again, the word used in Matthew 7: 24 is like unto the word that is used in Matthew 16: 18 **except** it has the definite article "*ten*" (την). This is the reason the New King James Version translates it as **the rock**. It refers to **Jesus** just as the word used in Matthew 16: 18. It is also the same word used in Matthew 27: 60 to describe the tomb where Jesus was laid that was hewn from **solid rock**! That promise in the **Sermon on the Mount** is backed by the guarantee of Jesus, the **Son of God**, who is eternal and had been with God from the beginning, who has all power in Heaven and in Earth! It was only six days later that Jesus took Peter, James and **John** atop the **Mount of Transfiguration** where all that He taught and promised was confirmed by a **voice from Heaven** that said, "*This is my beloved **Son**, in whom I am well pleased; **hear ye Him**.*" (Matthew 17: 5 KJV) Peter needed to hear those words because he had registered some doubt at Caesarea Philippi, to the extent that Jesus had to rebuke him. Later, other disciples like **Philip** and **Thomas** registered some doubt but never **John**!

131

Moreover, John took Jesus seriously when He said, "*Behold, I send the promise of My Father upon you: but **tarry ye** in the **city of Jerusalem**, until ye be **endued** with **power** from on high.*" (Luke 24: 49 KJV) When they were fishing after the resurrection, it was **John** who recognized Jesus after the big catch of fish and said to Peter, "*It is the Lord.*" (John 21: 7) John was present when Jesus imparted to them their missionary assignments in Acts 1: 8 just before His ascension. After His ascension, they returned to Jerusalem from Mount Olivet and they went into the Upper Room where Peter, James, and **John** abode. There they obeyed the Lord and continued "*with one accord in prayer and supplication*" until the power of the Holy Spirit fell upon them (Acts 1: 13-14).

Pentecost

This tremendous truth of God does not stop there. **John** was with the disciples on the day of Pentecost when the **church was born** and he participated. It was **John** who was with Peter and they were on their way up to the Temple at the hour of prayer when a lame man asked alms of them. It was **Peter and John** who fastened their eyes upon him and said, "*Look on us.*" (Acts 3: 4) Peter said, "*Silver and gold I do not have but what I do have I give to you. In the name of **Jesus Christ of Nazareth**, rise up and walk.*" John was with Peter on Solomon's porch when the lame man came holding on to Peter and John. It was **Peter and John** who were imprisoned for preaching the gospel to the people. It tells us something of their commitment when Luke tells us in Acts 4:13 that "*When they saw the boldness of **Peter and John**, and perceived that they were unlearned and ignorant men, they **marveled**; and they took **knowledge** of them that they had **been with Jesus**.*" (KJV)

When the apostles in Jerusalem heard that the people of Samaria had received the Word of God, it was Peter and **John** that they sent to investigate. When they saw that the people of Samaria had, indeed, received the gospel they laid hands on them and they received the **Holy Spirit**. (Acts 8: 14-17)

What Paul Says

It was the Apostle Paul who referred to **John** as one of the "**pillars**" of the **church at Jerusalem** (Galatians 2: 9). History is very clear that John pastored the church at Ephesus for 20 years before he was exiled, for his preaching, to the Isle of Patmos during the wicked rule of Domitian, the Roman Emperor, who severely persecuted Christians.

The first **epistle** of **John** is written to admonish Christians about how they should live, and it contains the elements of fellowship and assurance. In the fourth and fifth chapters of I John, he shares words of instruction, love, faith, victory, and confidence to the people of the **church**.

It is sad when there are people who abuse the church for their own personal agenda. There are charlatans who want to be "leaders" of the church and exercise influence. There are others who want to use the church for their own aggrandizement. There are those self-styled "church bosses" who continually bring broken fellowship, heartache, and grief to the church. John had to deal with such a person whose name was **Diotrephes**. He commended his friend, Gaius, and another friend by the name of Demetrius who, many scholars believe, was one of the silversmiths in Ephesus who lead a riot against the Christians but, apparently, was later converted himself (Acts 19: 24). Therefore, we see that there is evidence abounding that John was a part of the church and worked in the church as a pastor giving himself unreservedly to the task of the church (III John).

Letters to the Seven Churches

We have established that John was very active in the church from the day of its birth on the day of Pentecost. There came that time, as pointed out earlier, when he took the pastorate of the church at Ephesus where he served for about 20 years according to historical records. Now, John has been exiled on the Isle of Patmos because of his fidelity to the Word of God and because of his testimony about Jesus Christ.

In the very first verse of the first chapter, the source of the Revelation is named and it is **Jesus Christ**! Many scholars believe that this is the only book of the Bible that claims Jesus as the author and John as the scribe who wrote what the Lord commanded him to write. It was signified to **John** by an **angel** of the **Lord**. The instruction of the angel was, *"What you see, write in a book and send it to the seven churches which are in Asia ..."* (Revelation 1: 11)

John's Preparation to Write

It is obvious that our Lord is impressing upon John, in these preparation verses, the importance of the material that he is about to write. He is commanding John to write in a book what He reveals to him and send that message to the **seven churches**, which are in **Asia**. John had received a foretaste of Christ's glory atop the Mount of Transfiguration. There John saw Him visiting with heavenly visitors. There was Moses, the lawgiver and Elijah, the prophet. There was an overpowering radiance being emitted from Christ, Himself. There was the voice of the Father from Heaven confirming all that Jesus had taught.

However, here, as the triune God prepares John for the most important writing of his life, He takes **John** to the very **pinnacle of revelation**. It is an eternal glory that is being revealed to John.

It is the glory that He and the Father shared, *"before the world was."* (John 17:17) John had **witnessed** Him after the **resurrection** in His **glorified body** in which He could simply appear on the scene or even pass through closed doors (John 20: 19). Again, He appeared to **Cleopas** and another on the road to **Emmaus**. Obviously, He could transport Himself to distant places in a moment of time after the resurrection (Luke 24: 13-16). John was present when Jesus **ascended** to **Heaven**. What an experience that must have been! (Luke 24: 49-53; Acts 1: 8 - 11) The book that John is about to pen at the **direction of Jesus Christ** begins with beatitude when He said, *"Blessed is he that readeth, and they that **hear** the words of this **prophecy**, and keep those things which are written therein: for the time is at hand."* (Revelation 1: 3 KJV) Christ is presented as *"the **faithful witness**"* and *"the **first begotten of the dead**, and the **prince** of the kings of the earth."* (Verse 3) He is presented as the one who loved us and washed us from our sin with His own blood (Verse 5). He is also one who will **come in the clouds** as the angels indicated in the first chapter of Acts, *"And **every eye shall see Him**, even those who pierced Him and the people of the earth will wail when they see Him."* (Revelation 1: 7)

The Jewel

There is a jewel in verse 8 of the first chapter. Jesus is revealed as the **alpha** and the **omega**, the **beginning** and the **ending**. Alpha is the first letter of the Greek alphabet and the omega is the last. This means that the message of Jesus is **complete**. There is no other name among men whereby we must be saved (Acts 4: 12). It is not Jesus plus anything. He is **the** way, **the** truth and **the** life and **no one** can approach the Father except through Him. That is the most powerful and piercing message of John 14. The message of Buddha will not suffice; nor will the message of Hari

Krishna, Mohammed or any other mortal. **It is Jesus plus nothing**! One wag said that this verse concerning the beginning and the ending means that Jesus "is the whole ball of wax." That may be a colloquial way of putting it but there is a message there.

He Was In The Spirit

It is very important to note that when John received this message he was in the **Spirit on the Lord's Day** when he heard the great voice of the Lord that was like a trumpet. The trumpet symbol is to reveal to John how important the **message** is that he is about to receive. A great announcement is to be made. That is when **trumpets** were sounded. Something of grave importance is about to be released. When John heard the voice like a trumpet, he turned to see where the voice came from and when he turned he saw seven lamp-stands representing the seven churches. The lamp-stands give light and the oil in the lamp-stands is often associated with the presence of the Spirit. That reinforces the announcement that John was **in the Spirit** when he received this **message** (Verse 10). Walking among the lamp-stands was the Lord who is described as the "*Son of Man.*" This term harks back to Daniel 7:13 where the "*Son of Man*" is presented as the second person of the trinity and the Heavenly Father is presented as the "*Ancient of Days.*" The seven lamp-stands represent the seven churches that will receive these writings and the Lord, described as the "*Son of Man*" and clothed with a garment down to His feet with a golden girdle around His chest area, is walking among the lamp-stands as a **caretaker**! What a reaffirmation of Hebrews 7:25 where the Spirit has announced, "*He is able to save to the uttermost*" those who come to God through our Lord because "*He ever liveth*" to make intercession for us. Christ has not entered into the holy places made with men's hands, for they were only a figure of the truth. Rather, Christ, Himself, has entered into Heaven itself to appear in the presence of God **for us**. Again, it is confirmed unto us that *"there is one God, and **one mediator** between God and men, the man **Jesus Christ**."* (I Timothy 2: 5) This is a confirmation of what John had said in I John 2: 1 where he pointed out that we should not sin but *"if any man sin, we have an advocate with the Father, Jesus Christ the righteous ...."* (I John 2: 5) Why? Because, Jesus Christ offering up His own body for us was the **once for all** sacrifice for our sins. (Hebrews 10: 10)

The Bride

In Ephesians 5: 22 - 33 the church is presented as the **Bride of Christ** for which He died. The command is that just as Christ loved the church and gave Himself for it, then we are to love the church as we love our own bodies because the church is the body of Christ. Some are called as prophets, evangelists, and pastor-teachers for the perfecting of saints, for the work of the ministry and for the edifying of the body of Christ (Ephesians 4: 11-12). If Christ loved the church enough to give Himself for it and call out special ministers for the edifying of the church, should we not also love the church and minister as a part of the body of Christ? What a beautiful picture of the church as our Lord compares it to marriage

A Span of Time

Before John starts writing the letters to the seven churches, Jesus has made it clear to him that He is not only the one who was dead and is alive forevermore but that the things that he is going to write about will cover a long span of time. The command to John was, *"Write the things which you **have seen**, and the things **which are** and the things **which will take place after this**."* As best we can figure, John was above 90 years of age when he penned this book. He had seen a lot. At the time of this writing, Christians of the world were under Domitian persecution. He was to write about the things he was seeing and he would also write about things that **were** to come in the **future** (Revelation 1: 19). He also declares that the seven stars are the seven **angels** of the church. Angels were messengers. All scholars agree that the seven angels refer to the **pastors** (or messengers) of the churches. The lamp-stands refer to the **seven churches** and the Lord is mingling among them to take care of them.

The letters to the churches of Asia have multiple meanings. **First**, these letters will cover the entire church age from the **birth** of the church on the **day of Pentecost** until the time when the church is **caught out** of this world in the **rapture**. (II Thessalonians 4: 13 – 18) That is the **span of time** that is covered in these letters to the seven churches.

Seven particular churches are selected. There were many other churches but our Lord selected seven churches that represent the **predominant conditions** of churches during the time between its' founding and its' being caught away. Not only are there seven actual churches but each church represents the condition of the church in a particular age that is predominant. While these churches bear these characteristics at the time of these writings, there will be some churches in **every age** that will contain these characteristics and each age division will be **predominantly** represented by **one** of the **characteristics** of one of the seven churches.

We must remember these things as we study the letters to the seven churches.

Ephesus (Revelation 2: 1-7)

The church at Ephesus was a large church. **John** had pastored this church. It was founded by Paul. The church at Ephesus was born in the midst of turmoil. We read about its' beginning in the 19th chapter of Acts. When Paul arrived in Ephesus, he found a small group of believers. As for the men there were "about twelve" (Acts 19: 7). Most scholars believe that they were there because they were Jews who had gone to Jerusalem on the day of Pentecost and became believers on that day. That was true of the known world at that time because the people gathered at Jerusalem were from **all nations** of the known world. (Acts 2: 9-11) While they apparently had become believers, at that time, they had not been **fully instructed** and this was a great part of Paul's missionary journeys. They had only been baptized with the baptism of John, which was simply a baptism symbolizing repentance. Paul properly instructed them and baptized them in the name of **Jesus.** Afterward, he laid hands on them, they received the Holy Spirit, and a small Pentecost took place. They prophesied in **other languages** in which they had **not been instructed**.

Paul began teaching in the synagogue and remained there for about three months reasoning and persuading concerning the things of the Kingdom of God. The Jewish people of the synagogue were very hardened and began to speak evil of the "**way**" before the multitude. Therefore, Paul **ceased** to teach in the **synagogue** and began to teach in the school of **Tyrannous** (Acts 19: 8-9). He continued teaching there for two years and the Word of the Lord spread from there into most of Asia because Ephesus was the **chief city** of Asia (now known as Asia Minor).

God authenticated His Word through Paul by physical miracles, mostly miracles of healing. God so worked through him that even handkerchiefs or aprons, which had been on the body of Paul, were used to heal the sick.

Healing

It is good to remember at this point that there are two kinds of miracles. There are **physical miracles** and there are **spiritual miracles**. Some have the gift of **healing**. Luke, the writer of Acts, was a **physician**. Physical miracles are always used to **authenticate the Word of God**. It was James who said, *"Is any among you sick? Let him call for the **elders of the church**, and let them pray over him, anointing him with oil in the **name of the Lord**. And the prayer of faith will save the sick and the Lord will raise him up. And if he has committed sins, he will be forgiven."* (James 5: 14-15) Of course, we must always remember that the answer to our prayers is always to be conditioned by the will of God and that no one is going to live forever. Moreover, it is appointed unto man once to die and after that the judgment (Hebrews 9: 27). Even though Paul performed **great miracles** in Ephesus, the gift of healing was **not given indiscriminately**. Even the Apostle Paul left Trophimus at Miletus sick (II Timothy 4: 20). If Paul could have healed him, it is sure that he would have. Even Paul had an infirmity that God would not heal him of but gave him **grace** to bear it (II Corinthians 12: 7-10). It is not always the will of God that all people should be healed in every circumstance but we are thankful for those physicians, nurses, and paramedics who love God and work tirelessly to heal the sick. Moreover, we must always remember that **all healing is of God**. The surgeon may "set the stage" for the healing but it is the **Heavenly Father** who causes those cells to **knit back together** and heal. While **medications such as antibiotics** may diminish those things that prevent healing, it is always the works of **God that does the healing**.

IS THE CHURCH IMPORTANT?

Hezekiah

It is instructive to look at the life of Hezekiah who was a good King. God told him to put his house in order because he was about to die. He prayed and asked for God's healing and God added fifteen years to his life (Isaiah 38: 1-6) but he later died. This author believes in divine healing because he believes that all healing is divine but he believes that the greatest healing business in the world is **spiritual healing** or the healing of the soul. Yes, there is a balm in Gilead to heal the **sin sick soul** (Jeremiah 8: 22). Physical miracles are rare and temporary. Always they are given to strengthen belief in the person and power of the triune God. There was the parting of the waters at the Red Sea, the giving of the sweet water from the waters of Marah (Exodus 15: 25) and the manna from Heaven when the Children of Israel were in the Wilderness.

God's Rebuke

God **rebuked** the Israelites for their **forgetting** of the miracles that He did in Egypt and the Wilderness because they would not harken to His voice (Numbers 14: 22). There is a great example of the miracle atop Mount Carmel in the contest between Elijah and the prophets of Baal (II Kings 18: 37-38). There is the miracle of Jonah being swallowed by a whale and delivered safe to the seashore after which he preached repentance in Nineveh. It was a matter of God dealing with a reluctant prophet. Jesus spoke of this miracle in Matthew 12: 40. In the short time that Jesus ministered on earth, there were a great many miracles wrought by His hands. The first was the turning of water into wine in Cana of Galilee (John 2: 11). When He went up to Jerusalem to the Feast of the Passover, many **believed in His name** when they *"saw the signs which He did."* (John 2: 23) When **Nicodemus** came to Jesus by night to talk with him, he made clear that the basis of his desire to talk with Jesus was because of the **miracles that Jesus had performed** and he declared that no one could do those physical miracles except God be with him (John 3: 2). A great multitude followed Jesus because they saw His miracles (John 6: 2). Jesus, however, rebuked some of the people following the feeding of the multitude who sought Him, not because they had seen the **miracles** but because they **ate of the loaves and the fish** (John 6: 26).

Jesus gave a summary statement regarding His purpose for miracles when He received the news that Lazarus had died. At that point, He gave a strong statement regarding the purpose of physical miracles when He said, *"I am glad for **your sakes** that I was not there, that you **may believe.** Nevertheless let us go to him."* (John 11: 15) However, physical miracles are always temporary. Lazarus died again. The son of the widow of Nain was raised up from the dead but he later died. Again, we must emphasize that physical miracles are rare and are always temporary.

Spiritual Miracles

Spiritual miracles, however, last forever because the greatest of all spiritual miracles is **salvation.** There was His healing of the **demoniac** in Capernaum (Luke 4: 31-35). He dealt with a sinful woman at the house of Simon (Luke 7: 36-50). Who could forget His dealing with the **demoniac** of **Gadara** whose life was changed forever? The people came out and found the demoniac **clothed** and in "**his right mind**" (Mark 5: 1-20). There was the conversion of Zacchaeus that is indelibly imprinted upon the hearts and minds of Christians through the centuries. It was another great spiritual miracle (Luke 19: 1-10). There was the crowning miracle of all spiritual miracles that took place on the Damascus Road with the conversion of the Apostle Paul (Acts 9: 1-18). It is our purpose here to help the reader keep miracles in proper perspective. Spiritual miracles are for **eternity**!

Ephesian Miracles

It is obvious that God allowed Paul to perform miracles in Ephesus that people might believe and the church **grew very rapidly**. In fact, it grew so rapidly that a silversmith by the name of Demetrius called the other people of that trade together and said, "*... you see and hear that not only at Ephesus, but throughout almost all Asia this Paul has persuaded and turned away many people, saying that there are not gods which are made with hands. So that not only is this trade of ours in danger of falling into disrepute, but also the temple of the great goddess Diana may be despised and her magnificence destroyed whom all Asia and the world worship.*" (Acts 19: 23-28) There was a great tumult in Ephesus as a result of their protest.

Paul ministered at Ephesus for three years after the founding of the church and sometime later Paul went back to Miletus where he landed and summoned the elders of the Ephesian church. They were so large that they had many elders. Paul reviewed his ministry there with them and how he labored among them with many tears and trials. He reviewed the fact that he had given them the whole counsel of God and had not withheld anything from them. After his departure, "*savage wolves*" would come among them and **not spare the flock**. He cautioned that even among themselves there would be men who would rise up speaking perverse things and attempting to draw away disciples after themselves (Acts 19: 29-30). He charged them to be watchful and remember that for three years both night and day he did not cease to warn them with tears (Verse 31).

John's Pastorate at Ephesus

When John is writing to them, several years had passed. John had pastored there, as we have pointed out, for about 20 years. Now, he is exiled on the Isle of Patmos because of his loyalty to the gospel and to the Word of God. Our Lord has selected the Ephesian church as a representative church of the Apostolic Age. The Lord identifies Himself as the one who has total control because He has the *"seven stars in His right hand."* (Revelation 2: 1) There is much about the church during the Apostolic Age that pleased the Lord. They labored patiently for the sake of the Lord and they had not fainted (Revelation 2: 2). It was a working church. There were no drones.

They Had Discipline

The Ephesian church had not tolerated evil in its midst. They had discipline in their church. They would not tolerate members who were living double lives. If a member lived a life that brought reproach upon the church, the church would deal with them very emphatically. The church insisted on holy living. They were more concerned about the spiritual condition of the membership more than the size.

Again, we see the warnings of Paul come to fruition. They had **tested** those who came saying they were Apostles but they were not. They had found them to be liars (Revelation 2: 2). The Ephesian church was **sound in faith**. Phony preachers were not tolerated in their midst.

Further, they hated the deeds of the Nicolaitans, which the Lord also hated (Verse 6). Who were these people? The term Nicolaitans is made up of two words; one is "nikao" which means, "to conquer," and "iaos" which means "the people." Our word laity comes from it. The terms, obviously, are used to describe a system

144

that ultimately divided the church of our Lord into the groups that we call "the clergy" and "the laity." It was a system in which bishops and elders lorded it over the lay people of the church but the Ephesian church would have none of it. Our Lord said that He hates that sort of thing. The deeds of these Nicolaitans and their doctrine were rejected. It was a great church that had stood by the faith.

Something Is Wrong

However, in the midst of this commendation, our Lord, with those piercing, flaming eyes saw some things that were not in order. He said, *"Nevertheless I have this against you, that you have left your first love."* (Verse 4) They were still working hard but they were not working with the passion that they knew when they first found the Lord. The Lord's prescription was that they *"remember therefore from whence you have fallen; repent and do the first works or else I will come to you quickly and remove your lamp stand from its place unless you repent."* (Verse 5) Obviously, dissension and declension had already set in and there was only one cure for what had gone wrong.

Repentance

They must repent! Repentance does not always come easy. It means to cast away pride. It means to do an about face and walk in the opposite direction in some area of the church's life. It means to stop walking in the direction in which one is walking. They are to **return** to their **first love.** They are to regain that passion and zeal that they had in the beginning. In other words, the Ephesian Church needed **revival**. That is what happens in revival. Lives that are in a state of declension, discouragement, and depression **return** to the Lord. When that happens, grudges are set aside.

145

Animosities are gone. Pride is cast out of the believers' hearts and it is replaced with love. They are to return to the "first works" **or else**. What will happen if they fail to return? If they fail to repent, the Lord will remove the lamp stand. In other words, He will take away the church and it will no longer exist. Yes, the people will still gather there but the Holy Spirit will not be there. The church will be dead. They may still light candles and sing hymns but the church will be dead. A layman described one such church as a church "where the furnace was still blowing air but the fire was out." This condition began to affect the church not only during the Apostolic Age but there would be some churches of every age that would suffer this same malady that became characteristic of the church during the Apostolic Age. We still see this condition in our day. It is still true that this condition can only be remedied by **repentance** and return to the teachings of the Lord and receiving of the power of the Holy Spirit. **May it be so**!

Smyrna: the Persecuted Church (Revelation 2: 8-11)

The Lord's message to the Smyrna church was one of encouragement and commendation. Smyrna had been a very prosperous city at one time and then, for all practical purposes, it died. It was rebuilt by Alexander the Great and Antigonus. Then it became a strategic and wealthy city and was a significant center of wealth and commerce during the New Testament era. The church may have been planted when Paul was at Ephesus and sending Christians from Ephesus to bear witness in Smyrna. The one thing that stands out in history concerning Smyrna was that the great, respected preacher, Polycarp, was martyred there. He may have well been pastor of the church at Smyrna when the letter was written to them.

Time Period

Many students of the New Testament believe that the Smyrna church represents the period of the first and second centuries to AD 316. The period has sometimes been called the "Martyr Period." During that time, thousands of Christians sealed their faith by their death at the sword of their tormentors. There was a time when Christians did not worship in great cathedrals or palatial edifices but they often worshipped and lived in places like the catacombs where many Christians were born and died without ever seeing the light of day.

When Polycarp was martyred, his friends had persuaded him to hide away on a farm but the pagan fanatics found him and tried to force him to recant his faith. He had a faith that was unshakeable and was born of faith in the Son of God. His answer to them was, *"Eighty and six years have I served my Lord, and He has been my truest friend. How then can I blaspheme Him who shed His blood to wash away my sins?"* He was burned at stake but in his dying moments, he yielded up the spirit that sustained him while his body was being turned to ashes. As John communicates the Lord's comforting message to that church, John's kindness and tenderness shines through in the words that he pens. The introduction to the Lord's message was: *"These things says the first and the last, who was dead and came to life ..."* (verse 8)

The Lord's first message to them was one of assurance as He reminded them that *"I know your works, tribulation, and poverty (but you are rich); and I know the blasphemy of those who say they are Jews and are not, but are a synagogue of Satan."*

These suffering Christians have lost everything including all their material possessions but the Lord assures them that they are *"rich."* Any person who has been saved by the shed blood of Christ is rich regardless of what status he may hold in the world. A story comes to us from yesteryear when a slave received Christ as His

Savior. He said, "In Christ I own everything. The sun is mine. I can sit in it. The air is mine. I can breathe it. The earth is mine. I can lie down in it." In other words, he was saying, "When I have Christ I have everything that I need to sustain me for time and eternity." He believed that Christ was sufficient for all of man's needs.

The Lord's Comforting Words

This Scripture comes alive when the people of Smyrna who have suffered so much hear the Lord introduce Himself as the ***"first and the last"*** and ***"the one who was dead and is alive."*** He is promising the people of Smyrna that, regardless of how much they have suffered and what losses they have sustained, there will be a day when **He will make all things right**.

What comfort and encouragement to the people of Smyrna and the period of the martyrs when He said, "*I know your works, tribulation, and poverty.*" That word, "tribulation" is a word that came from Roman farmers. It was a wooden paddle fastened to the end of a pole with a leather thong. The Romans did not use oxen or any other animal to tread out their grain. They took that tribulum and beat the grain on the thrashing floor until all of the grain had come through. Our word "tribulation" comes from that word. When the world is beating down upon you with all it has and it seems that everyone in the world has forgotten you, Christ is there by your side to say, "I know."

Even in the midst of their horrible persecution they stood by their beliefs and Jesus commends them for it when He says, "*I know the blasphemy of those who say they are Jews and are not, but are a synagogue of Satan.*"

More Suffering

There will be more suffering in the future and our Lord comforts them by saying: "Do not fear any of those things which you are about to suffer. Indeed the Devil is about to throw some of you into prison, that you may be tested, and you will have tribulation ten days. Be faithful unto death, and I will give you the **crown of life**." (Verse 10) The crown of life is one that goes to those who endure and "...have been proved." (James 1: 12) It goes to those who love the Lord. Every believer will be tested at some time or other in his life. It is only the Lord who can help us through those periods of temptation and give us victory. John makes it clear in Revelation 2: 11 that this message is coming through the **Spirit**. Jesus knows all about it because He was the one whom Paul describes as one who was rich but for our sakes, He became poor so that we, through His poverty, could be made rich (II Corinthians 8: 9). These people, though they were suffering physically, received blessings of God beyond measure as the Holy Spirit ministered to them in their time of need.

The Ten Days

The Lord warned them that the Devil would cast some of them into prison and they would be tried and that they would have tribulation for ten days. This was the message to Smyrna. The word Smyrna means "myrrh." It was an ingredient for embalming the dead and was used when Jesus was buried. It was also one of the spices that the Wise Men brought to Jesus at the time of His birth. It was almost a prophesy at His birth as to how He would leave this life. To those who are faithful unto to death, Christ, with His nail pierced hands, will place upon them the **Crown of Life**. The word in Acts 1: 8 that is translated **witnesses** is "martures" (ναρτυρες). Our word "martyr" comes from the word. It means that Jesus was commissioning us to *"**bear testimony unto death**."* Many Christians at Smyrna and through the ages have given their lives because of their unfailing witness of Jesus Christ unto death.

Ten Days of Persecution

The Ten Days of Tribulation that the saints of Smyrna were to go through referred to ten specific edicts that the Roman government had issued in their attempt to stamp out Christianity. It was costly and sometimes life threatening in those days to be a Christian. Some were put into the arena to fight gladiators. Some were placed in the arena to be torn by lions. Some were tied to stakes around Nero's garden and were actually made into human torches around his gardens. Yes, it was costly and dangerous to be a Christian in those days. We see those days approaching again.

Pergamos: Satan's Headquarters (Revelation 2: 12-17)

Pergamos was the capitol city of the providence and the chief city in which the "Concilia," which was in charge of the state religion and emperor worship, was located. The city had always been very loyal to Rome and therefore was very hostile to Christianity. They were very vicious and unrelenting in their persecution of Christians. It is not certain but many scholars believe that the church was planted from the church at Ephesus or that it may have been established by some who were present on the Day of Pentecost. It was a very wealthy, cultured city.

The Lord identifies Himself as one with the *"sharp two edged sword."* (Revelation 2: 12) The sword is a **weapon** with which battle is done. The church is to understand that the Lord is prepared to do battle unless changes are made in the church. The message is that the Lord is prepared to do battle with **those in the**

church who are promoting error and immorality. Because the church is located in such a prominent city of emperor worship, it is described as the place where *"Satan's throne is."* There had been many martyrs in the church and the martyrdom of Antipas is probably a reference to the pastor of the church or some other outstanding member. It represents a period of history that began around 316 AD. The Lord commends those in the church who have **remained faithful** even, in the times of severe persecution

Compromise

Some in the church had no stomach for the persecution that was being unleashed against the faithful Christians. They suffered from the "let's all get along" syndrome. They were willing to trade off material and monetary gain for the loss of spiritual vitality.

It was about this time that Constantine came to the throne and made Christianity a state religion. Legend stated that Constantine had a dream of a fiery cross burning in the sky and heard a voice saying, "By this sign conquer." Learning that the cross was the symbol of the Christian church, he joined the Christian church but probably he was never truly converted. However, he became an instrument to bring about an unholy alliance between the church and the world. At one time, there was a coin in the British museum that was issued under the rule of Constantine. On one side, there was a Christian emblem and on the other side, there were emblems of the pagan gods. Constantine took the name of "Pontifex Maximus" which means the "High Priest of all religions." He commanded that Christian persecutions cease and that many heathen temples should be converted into Christian churches. By the time of his reign, Christians had begun to number in the millions. Of course, Pergamos was corrupt in every way. The famous temple of Aesculapius was located in Pergamos. He was the Greek god of healing. Thousands of harmless snakes inhabited the area around the temple. People came from all over the empire seeking healing at the temple.

Moreover, it was at Pergamos that parchment was first used as a writing material. It was at Pergamos that the Attalid kings built a huge library of more than 200,000 volumes.

Balaam

The Lord issues a complaint against the people in the Pergamos church because some of them had swallowed the doctrine of Balaam. You read about it in Numbers 22 - 25. Balak was a Moabite king. The Children of Israel were on their way from Egypt to the Promised Land. Balak feared confrontation with them. He sent for a prophet by the name of Balaam. He bribed Balaam to place a curse on Israel. While he was on his way, an angel of the Lord stood in front of him and Balaam's donkey crushed his foot against the wall of a vineyard trying to get around the angel. The donkey balked and Balaam struck him three times with his stick. The donkey balked because the donkey could see the angel even though Balaam could not see him. The donkey said, *"What have I done to you, that you have struck me these three times?"* Balaam answered the donkey, *"Because you have abused me. I wish there were a sword in my hand, for now I would kill you!"* The donkey answered Balaam, *"Am I not your donkey on which you have ridden ever since I became yours, to this day? Was I ever disposed to do this to you?"* Balaam said, *"No."* It was then that the Lord opened Balaam's eyes. Even though Balaam tried several times to curse the Children of Israel, he was not able to do it.

The Children of Israel, however, began to commit immorality with the daughters of Moab and they did it according to the counsel of Balaam (Numbers 31: 16). Now, the people of Israel had lost their testimony and they could no longer consider themselves a separated people from the sins of the pagans.

At Pergamos

This kind of thing happened at Pergamos. Bishops became ruthless rulers and princes of the state became heads of the church. There was an unholy union between the professing church and the pagans. God's charge to the church was *"repent; or else!"* (Revelation 2:16) God warned them that if they continued in their sinful ways He would come to them quickly and fight **against them**. There would be no more delay in His judgment that would fall upon the church.

His Promise

His promise to those who would remain faithful was that He would give unto them of the **hidden manna** (a blessing that no one could even imagine) and He would give them a white stone that would have a new name written upon it for those who would receive it. Just as the needs of the Children of Israel in the wilderness were divinely provided, so the Lord would provide for the needs of those who were faithful unto death. It will be a sustenance that the world could not understand. The white stone was something that was native to the area. Perhaps it was like white Carrera marble. It was given for several reasons:

1. The white stone was given to men who had been falsely accused and tried but acquitted of any crime and the stone would forever declare their innocence.
2. The white stone was also given to men who had been freed from slavery and made citizens. The stone was an indication of their citizenship and freedom.
3. Sometimes, the stone was given to the winner of a sports contest or a race as an indication that they had overcome in their competition with the world.

4. Sometimes, the stone was given to a soldier returning from battle after victory over the enemy.

Government Encroachment

It has been true in almost every century that the state has tried to encroach upon the church. In America, after oppression in the early days, we became free from state control or established churches because of the First Amendment to our Constitution. Now, the state is encroaching upon the church again. Zoning laws are limiting access to churches. Increasingly, Christian ministers are being forbidden to mention Christ in the public square. People who are supposed to be Christian are living together unmarried. They bear children who are confused about their identity and their morality. There are groups of atheists that are being formed who are pressing for churches to be taxed. For instance, the Associated Press reported that on April 2, 2012 for the first time in history, the U.S. military hosted an atheist event expressly for soldiers and others who do not believe in God with a county fair-like gathering on the main parade ground at one of the world's largest Army Posts. Sgt. Justin Griffith, local organizer of the event, is the Military Director of the American Atheists organization. The group was hoping for a crowd of about 5,000. The report stated that "several hundred" showed up. The notorious English Atheist, Richard Dawkins of Oxford said, "We're not antagonistic toward religious believers, but we're antagonistic toward religious beliefs." The gathering took place on the parade ground at Fort Bragg, North Carolina. On the same day that this AP report was issued there was an article and picture about a gay pride flag being raised over a U.S. Military Base in Afghanistan instead of the Stars and Stripes. What are we coming to as a Nation?

Christians need to be alerted to this sort of thing because the power to tax is the power to destroy. It must have grieved the heart of John to pen these words but John knew that there could not be compromise or the church would be lost. Pastors who call for separated living are often persecuted. The anti-God fanatics of the world often mention only one phrase of the First Amendment and they ignore the second phrase, which declares that the free exercise of religion will not be prohibited. Babies are being killed in the womb and they call it the Mother's "choice."

The world was shocked when the Fox News Channel reported on June 17, 2010, that the Veterans Memorial Elementary School of Provincetown, Massachusetts was distributing condoms to those young **elementary** students. This kind of thing is done in the name of sex education. When will Americans say: "**Enough is enough!**"

Doctrine of Balaam

As we ponder the condition of Pergamos where there were people who taught the doctrine of Balaam with all its' moral corruption and denial of faith along with the doctrine of the Nicolaitans which represented ecclesiastical authority over the laymen, we have to wonder if the condition of America is much better. Some of the Christians at Pergamos had compromised their faith in exchange for security and recognition by the world. Again, we learn that bad belief equals bad conduct. In America, we have professing Christians who live openly in adultery. Pastors are being asked to pray at public meetings without mentioning the name of Jesus Christ. It is a sad thing that pastors are asked to do this but it is even more serious because too many pastors comply under the pretense that they will have **some witness** when, in fact, they have destroyed their witness by compromising the **name of Jesus!** Are we any better than the people of Pergamos? As we pen this book, Christians running for government office are being criticized for being Christians. At a state university, the students in one class were required to read the **Koran** but not the **Bible**. Day after day Christians are **intimidated** into silence.

Why did the Lord choose Pergamos and direct John to write about it? Because He knew that Pergamos would be characteristic of the third and fourth centuries and that there would be churches in every century that would be like Pergamos. The Lord makes it clear that He will come and fight against any church that compromises as did the church at Pergamos. The world will always welcome you if you want to go their way but do not expect them to adopt anything that you believe or even give you any sympathy. May our Lord **deliver Americans from the spirit of Pergamos.**

Thyatira: An Immoral Church (Revelation 2: 18-29)

There is no record of how or when the church at Thyatira was founded. It could have been founded by someone from the Ephesian church. Like others, it could have been founded by someone from the Day of Pentecost or someone like Lydia, the seller of purple who lived in that city. It was on a Roman trade route, which ran on to Pergamos. It was visited by many people. The same heresy that was prominent at Pergamos was present at Thyatira only it appeared to be worse. The city was teeming with immoral, pagan people and immorality quickly took root there.

Christ identifies Himself as the "Son of God." He is infallible, omniscient, and omnipotent. His piercing eyes were like a flame of fire. Nothing is hidden from Him. The feet of brass in Holy Scripture are often used to remind us of strength and judgment. The person speaking to the church is not a person who does not matter. He is the Son of God who matters very much about **everything**. Every Christian needs to understand that He still matters!

Things That Please Him

The Lord just does not give a blank condemnation to the church at Thyatira. There are some things that some of the people are doing that please Him. It is a working church and, unlike Ephesus, they work out of love (Revelation 2:19). They perform services to others. They are motivated by faith. They are patient. As to their works, they are growing in those works. "The last are more than the first." There is obviously a core of very dedicated people at the church in Thyatira and the Lord commends them. They are not only dedicated but they are a patient people.

The Lord's Displeasure

Some things about the church were very displeasing to the Lord. The Lord's complaint against the church does not involve that core of Christians in the church who were faithful in their work and service. It was because of what they **tolerated**. There was a person in the church that the Lord refers to as "**Jezebel**." She may have had such a name but it is the opinion of most scholars that the woman is called "Jezebel" because of the things that she advocated. She was sexually immoral and taught others to be immoral. Some scholars believe that she was the pastor's wife. She apparently is very prominent in the church. Some scholars have translated the phrase, "*that woman Jezebel*" as "*your wife Jezebel*" which would refer to the pastor's wife because the root word from which "woman" is translated is "gune" (γυνή). Most translations have avoided this because it does not seem very plausible to them. It is likely that the "Jezebel" referred to is harking back to the Old Testament character that persecuted the prophets of God. The prophets of Baal ate at her table and Obadiah took a hundred prophets of God and hid them in caves by 50, feeding them bread and water to sustain them. Jezebel was the daughter of Ethbaal, king of the Zidonians. She was a worshipper of Baal and Ahab worshipped with her. He built a house of Baal in Samaria and established an altar therein. We read about the exploits of Jezebel in I Kings 16 -22. We read about her death in II Kings 9. She was actually a ruthless person who brought immorality and pagan worship into Israel, the Northern Kingdom.

The Sin

The sin of the church at Thyatira was the sin of tolerance. They had allowed Jezebel to function as a "prophetess" and who taught sexual immorality and the eating of things sacrificed to idols. The Lord had given her time to repent but she did not repent. One of the saddest and most incomprehensible things we see in church life is the willingness of many churches to tolerate sin and debauchery in the membership and sometimes among the leadership. They sometimes flaunt their sin and rebellion before the other members of the congregation. A paradigm has developed among Christian churches that "tolerance" is always good. That is not necessarily true. In some ways, tolerance may be good but in many ways, it is wickedness and evil that destroys the testimony of the church. As a teenager, this writer had a Sunday School teacher who was known to gamble all week and teach a Sunday School class on Sunday. I was the class secretary, took up the offering envelopes, and checked the roll on Sundays. The gentleman once gave me a dollar bill and asked me to bring him some change. I went to the church office and got two half dollars. When I brought them back to him, he asked me if I could not get it any smaller. He was not willing to give even a fifty-cent piece to the church but he was teaching teen-age boys. That bothered me tremendously.

Our Nation

Many in our Nation were recently shocked when the *New York Times* published the account of a homosexual wedding in our nation's capitol between the Press Secretary for the Speaker of the House of Representatives and the Vice-President for development at the Gay and Lesbian Victory Fund in Washington. A minister from the World Christian Fellowship Ministries officiated at the wedding. It was the disgusting case of a man marrying a man and the wedding being performed in our nation's capitol by one who calls himself a Christian minister. Is that any better than Baal worship, which became so popular because it condoned sexual immorality and was even a part of their worship? It is flabbergastingly amazing how so many will flock to a religion that is willing to compromise on moral principles. The Thyatira church is a representative of the Dark Ages from about 500AD to about 1500AD but there have been churches like Thyatira in every age. The characteristics of the Dark Ages were churches that lived in opulence and finery. While there were some sincere Christians in the church, beneath the surface was unbelievable corruption. The sin of immorality is something that every church must contend with in every age lest it become dominant throughout church life.

The Lord's Judgment

The Lord gave Jezebel space to repent but she repented not. This judgment is that He will cast her into the sickbed and those who commit adultery with her into great tribulation unless they repent of their sins. Immorality always takes a great toll on the human body. It is a great price that our God exacts from those who choose to abuse their bodies in immorality. Such diseases are rampant in America and thousands upon thousands of lives have been claimed by these terrible diseases. Many times people who engage in adultery and fornication try to tell themselves that medications are available that will cure venereal diseases and so many times they are shocked to learn that some of those terrible diseases are incurable. This is what the Lord is talking about when He says that He will cast Jezebel into a sickbed, which indicates a deathbed, and those who have participated in adultery with her will experience great tribulation unless they repent of their sins. The Lord promises that He will *"kill her children with death"* (Verse 23). He states very clearly that all the *"churches shall know that I am He who searches the minds and hearts. And I will give to each one of you according to your works."*

The Lord's Comfort

It is not all condemnation. The Lord says to those faithful Christians: "And to the rest in Thyatira, as many as do not have this doctrine, and who have not known the depths of Satan as they call them, I will put on you no other burden." (Verse 24) Those faithful Christians are not going to suffer more. He simply challenges them to hold fast what they have until He comes. To those who remain faithful and overcome, the Lord will "give power over the nations." This is a continuing theme of what Jesus established in Matthew 19: 28-29 when He assured His followers that "in the regeneration, when the Son of Man sits on the throne of His glory, you who have followed me will also sit on twelve thrones, judging the twelve tribes of Israel. And everyone who has left houses or brothers or sisters or father or mother or wife or children or lands, for My name's sake shall receive a hundred fold, and inherit everlasting life."

What are they to do now? They are to "hold fast" until He comes. He will also furnish the "morning star" which is a sign of God's unmistakable guidance. What a promise! It does not get any better than that! Jesus loved them enough to tell them the truth and John was faithful enough to record it accurately. Again, Jesus speaks powerfully through the great apostle John.

Sardis: Living In the Past (Revelation 3: 1-6)

Sardis was once a premiere city of Asia Minor. The word Sardis means, "Escaping." The city was bounded on three sides by precipitous cliffs. It was necessary to defend the city from only one side thus making it easy to defend. However, the city had grown careless and complacent when Croesus was king and was besieged by Cyrus. He and his soldiers were asleep, thinking themselves to be safe, when the city was sacked at night by the enemy. A similar thing happened under Achneus. The city was once again sacked by Antiochus the Great in the same manner.

During the Roman period, Sardis had lost its' prestige and the time to which John was writing, represented a period of a broken down aristocracy. They were still trying to live in the aristocracy of the past and could not accept the fact that the past was past. The church had taken on the personality of the city and they were facing the prospect of either awakening or dying.

Jesus Identifies Himself

In addressing the church at Sardis, Jesus identifies Himself through the **Apostle John** as the one who *"has the seven spirits of God and the seven stars."* At this point, He reveals something very startling when He says, *"I know your works, that you have a name that you are alive, **but you are dead.**"* (Revelation 3: 1) Of course, the church was still going through the motion. They were maintaining that reputation that they were *"alive"* but there was nothing of the **Spirit of God** in their worship and ministry. They were trying to live on their past glory. While they could speak much of their past glory, they could say little of what was

161

happening in the present. This is a sad thing to happen to any church and Sardis is not the last church to fall into this pattern. What they thought was beautiful **ritualism** had become nothing more than **rutualism**. A rut has been described as a grave with both ends out. Phony aristocracy has never done anything constructive for the Kingdom of God because the emphasis is always on the individual instead of God. It is a kind of religious **pride** that knows no bounds.

Sardis Is Different

There is a marked difference in the Lord's speaking to the church at Sardis and in His speaking to previous churches. In addressing other churches, He commended them first and then issued His complaint but at Sardis, there was little that was commendable. He, therefore, opens with His complaint. Their activity was not accompanied by the ministry of the Holy Spirit. It was simply human activity. There was no real spiritual life there. Jesus pronounced them "dead." There is an old western proverb that says, *"There are few things better organized than a graveyard, but there is no life there."* That is the way it was at Sardis. Without doubt, they were strong about observing past traditions but the omnipotent and omniscient one who could see the past, the present and the future diagnosed the church as being **dead**!

It is quite probable that the church was established by Christians who had been saved at Pentecost. They returned to establish the church there at Sardis. It was a heady time in Christianity when they established the church at Sardis. It was a time when Christians were viewed as a people who had *"turned the world upside down."* (Acts 17: 6) Now, however, they were simply living on past tradition.

The Remedy

However, our Lord did not leave this church in a lurch; He provided a remedy. Instead of the church living in the past and directing their energies to remembering and preserving the past, they should *"be **watchful and strengthen** the things which remain **that are ready to die.**"* While they were **working,** the Lord had not found their works **perfect** in the **eyes of God**.

In years past, the city had been sacked twice because they were not watchful. They were sacked by the enemy. What was the Lord saying to them? He is saying, *"be watchful because what has happened to the city in the **past** can happen to your church **today.**"* Instead of living in the past they are to *"**strengthen** the things that **remain**"* in the present. In other words, He is calling upon the people of the church at Sardis to emphasize the truly important and spiritual matters. Just as the **city** had an enemy in the **past**, the church has an **enemy**. Peter warned them about the enemy when he said, *"Be vigilant; because your **adversary** the **Devil** walks about **like a roaring lion**, seeking whom he may devour. **Resist** him, steadfast in the faith, knowing that the same sufferings are experienced by your brotherhood in the world."* (I Peter 5: 8-9) Therefore, does the Lord warn the people at Sardis to *"be watchful, and strengthen the things which remain **that are ready to die.**"*

Moreover, the Lord warns them to **remember** how they have **received** and how they have heard about the things of God and they are **to repent**. They are also to be watchful and alert for evil in their midst or else the Lord will come at a time that they do not expect, like a thief comes when he is least expected.

Commendations

Even in Sardis, there are some who have not *"defiled their garments."* They will walk with the Lord in **white** garments. That indicates that they will have **intimate fellowship** with the Lord. The **white garments** refer to lives of **purity** and their names will never be blotted out from the *"book of life"* but the Lord will confess them before the Father and before the angels. This is their wondrous reward for Godly living.

The Scope of This Teaching

Why did the Lord give us this teaching about an inconspicuous church by the name of Sardis? It is because the characteristics that were destroying Sardis have been prominent throughout history and He knew the **nature of man**. There was a period of history when this kind of religious malady spread like a plague among the churches of Europe and America. It was a time when religious **leaders** were exalted more than **Christ was**. The churches became stiff and formal. Ceremony took the place of regeneration. Churches were memorialized and honored more than Christ. Many of the great men of God who were memorialized in such a way would spin in their graves if they knew the spiritual condition of churches that were named after them and things that were done in these same **churches**. The Reformation that started so well became lifeless and burdened down with **human tradition** rather than proclaiming the cross and the empty tomb. The warning to Sardis is applicable today to those churches that have forgotten their **purpose and ministry** and are living in the past.

Thank God for those people in a church with lifeless ceremonies, who continue to **pray** and **stand** by the **faith** even though they are a minority. They can be sure that their names will never be blotted out from the **Book of Life** but rather their names will be ever before the **Father** and the **angels**.

Philadelphia: The Church of Brotherly Love (Revelation 3: 7 – 13)

The church at Philadelphia was probably the most famous of any of the seven churches. Sometimes scholars refer to it as "the church of the open door" but it became the church of the open door because it was first a **church of brotherly love**. The name has inspired men and women across the ages and around the world. Wherever Christendom has gone, there have been churches, villages, towns and cities that have been named Philadelphia. Many scholars always associate this church with the **modern missionary movement**, which began more than 200 years ago with William Carey. He was an English shoe cobbler when he published his first pamphlet in 1792, which is often called the **Missionary Manifesto** of the modern missionary movement. After he sensed the call of God, he constantly studied at his workbench. When he approached the pastors of London concerning his vision to take the Gospel to the heathen, he was told, "When God wants to convert the heathen, He will do it without assistance from you." Of course, most of those pastors were strict Calvinists and they were not really open to missionary involvement at that time.

The city dates back to about 159 BC. It got its' name from Attalus II whose loyalty to his brother Eumenes won him the epithet **philadelphus** which means "**brother lover**." It was founded as a Greek culture center whose people were intent on spreading the Greek language. It was a missionary city for the Hellenistic philosophy.

When the Lord addresses the church He identifies Himself as the **one who is holy and true** (verse 7). Not only is the Lord the

165

holy and true but He holds the **key of David**. This harks back to Isaiah 22: 22. Of course, Jesus was of the house and lineage of David (Luke 1: 27). This verse indicates that both **Mary** and **Joseph** were of the house and lineage of David and they were 28 generations from David (Matthew 1: 17). Because of His position with the Father and as a part of the **Godhead**, He can **open doors** that no one **can shut** and He can shut doors that no one can open. Again, **John** has faithfully recorded Jesus' teaching that He is the door to the sheepfold and if anyone enters in by **Him** he will be **saved** and the needs of his heart will be supplied (John 10: 7-9).

Opening and Shutting

Paul experienced the **opening** and **shutting** of doors by the Lord because the Lord always works through **His Holy Spirit**. After he had left Lystra, Paul wanted to preach the Gospel in the Roman province of **Asia** but the **Holy Spirit** forbad him. He then wanted to go to **Bithynia** and preach the Gospel there but the **Spirit** did not permit him. From there he went to **Troas** where he had a vision in the night in which he saw a man from Macedonia standing before him saying, "*Come over into Macedonia and help us.*" (Acts 16: 9) When Paul wrote to the Corinthians about it, he told them about his experience in Troas where he said, "*a door was open to me by the Lord.*" (II Corinthians 2: 12) The Lord had shut two doors and he could not open them but when the Lord opened the door to Macedonia, no one could shut it or prevent him from going. It was on that second missionary journey when the great church at Philippi was founded as well as the church at Thessalonica that account for two books of the New Testament. He was forbidden and had the door shut when he wanted to go to Asia and Bithynia because God knew what was awaiting him there and he likely would have ended his ministry there if he had disobeyed the Lord.

An Open Door

When closing out the first letter to the church at Corinth Paul said, "...I will tarry in Ephesus until Pentecost for a **great** and **effective door** has been **opened** to me, and there are many adversaries." (I Corinthians 16: 9) When Paul returned from his first missionary journey to Antioch, he reported to them all the mighty works they had been able to perform through the power of the **Holy Spirit** and his report said that God had "... **opened the door** of faith to the Gentiles." (Acts 14: 27) Sometimes, the Lord through His Holy Spirit opens the door to opportunity for witnessing and closes the door where we will be hindered or unsuccessful even though we may not understand it at the time. These Biblical examples provide a graphic illustration of times when God shuts doors that no man can open and opens doors that no man can shut. This is the reason that Christians must constantly seek the guidance of the **Holy Spirit** in their service to God.

The Meaning

Thus, we understand the meaning of the "*open door*" and God promises to the church at Philadelphia, even though they have just "*a little strength*," they have kept His word and **have not denied His name** (Verse 8). Upon that basis, God makes a promise to them saying, "*I know your works. See, I have set before you an open door, and no one can shut it, for you have a little strength, have kept My word, and have not denied My name.*" God will give them protection and turn the hearts that were of the synagogue of Satan, claiming themselves to be Jews but are not. Eventually, they will worship at the feet of the faithful and they will know that God has loved the people of the **Philadelphia** church.

Because the people of this church have kept the Lord's command, He will keep them from the hour of trial that will come upon the entire earth (Verse 10). He urges them to hold fast to what they have so that no one can take their crown. He will *"come quickly"* (or suddenly) and those who have been **found faithful** will have a permanent place in the temple of God and they will have a place in the new Jerusalem (Verse 12).

Laodicea: The Lukewarm Church (Revelation 3: 14 – 22)

Laodicea was a center for commerce throughout the region. When it was damaged by an earthquake about 60 AD, they needed no help from the Roman treasury. Three main trade routes from Rome converged at Laodicea thus making it an outstanding city for commerce and wealth. The word Laodicea literally means "the voice of the people." There was a certain amount of lethargy in the city that was caused by its' exceeding wealth and this same spirit had made its' way into the church. The church was lukewarm because instead of listening to the Word of **God**; the church was listening to the people and the church was conducting itself as **man** wanted the church to be conducted. When a church succumbs to the word of man instead of the Word of God, it is always a disgraceful thing to God. Man's words will pass away but the Word of God will stand **forever**!

The Lord Identifies Himself

Jesus identifies Himself as the Amen (άμεν). The word was transitioned from Hebrew to Greek to English without translation. Originally, the term referred to building up or nursing. It came to refer to that which was stable and positive – something that was unshakable and absolutely true. Jesus further identifies Himself as the alpha and the omega. These are the names of the first and last letters of the Greek alphabet. As we pointed out in the first chapter, Jesus was a part of the Godhead that was active in creation (John 1: 3). He is also the omega or the end of all things earthly. The Apostle Paul insisted that *"He is the image of the invisible God, the first born over all creation. For by Him all things were created that are in heaven and that are on earth, visible and invisible, whether thrones or dominions or principalities or powers. All things were **created** through Him and for Him and He is **before all things**, and in Him all things **consist.**"* (Colossians 1: 15 – 18) That word consists means that He **sustains everything** that we see in the earth. It also continues to state that He is the *"head of the body, who is the beginning, the first born from the dead, and that in all things He may have the pre-eminence."*

Moreover, He declares Himself as the *"faithful and true witness."* (Revelation 3: 14)

Shocking Revelation

Jesus then declares, "I know your works, that you are neither cold nor hot, I would wish you were cold or hot. So then, because you are lukewarm, and neither hot nor cold, I will spew you out of my mouth." (Verses 15 -16) It must have been startling to the people in Laodicea, that even though they may hide their condition from the eyes of men they could not hide it from God. He knows their intimate thoughts and our Lord announces that fact to them. Toward the Lord, they were lukewarm or tepid. It was a sickening thing to the Lord and He felt like spewing (vomiting) them out of His mouth. This was familiar to them. In nearby Hierapolis there were several beautiful springs of water. Often, travellers weary from their journey across the desert would stop, seeking water to quench their thirst but the water from those beautiful springs was lukewarm mineral water, and nothing was much more distasteful than that. The Lord is pointing out that the same condition exists in the Laodicean church.

The people in the church did not even understand their condition. They thought they had become wealthy and had need of nothing and they did not even realize that they were "wretched, miserable, poor, blind and naked..." (Verse 17)

The Diagnosis

Jesus' diagnosis of their condition was that they were in need of everything that they did not have. They were wretched and miserable. This often happens to people who are consumed by their wealth. They were actually poor, blind, and naked or, in other words, the world could clearly see their condition even as the Lord could see it but they did not even know what their condition was because they were so **blinded** by their **self-interest**.

The city was widely known for three principal enterprises. It was a city of banking because of so much mercantile trade. It was also a center for glossy black wool production, which was much more valuable than any other kind of wool. There was no need to dye this wool. It was also a center where medicines were made. One of the well-known medicines that were made in Laodicea was an **eye salve** that was very popular among travelers who had been travelling in desert conditions. It gave great comfort to the eyes.

The Lord's Counsel

The Lord's counsel to them is that in spite of their smugness before the world and the belief that their sins *"to men's eyes were hidden"* they were actually naked before the world. The Lord is counseling them that they need a **white robe,** not a black one made from fine wool. White indicates purity. They need to be robed in purity not in the black robes of haughty **self-sufficiency** because that would not cover their sins before God. The Lord also reminds them that they are **blind** and they need to have a **spiritual salve** that will heal the blindness of their eyes so they can see what their actual condition is. They needed **gold** that was refined by fire. In other words, their wealth needed to be refined before God. Some of it, undoubtedly, had been dishonestly obtained through sleazy and underhanded processes. Their wealth needed to be gained with purity and thus presented to the Lord. Jesus reminds them that He rebukes and chastens those whom He loves and He, therefore, calls upon them to **repent.** The Lord's chastening is also very much emphasized in Hebrews 12: 5-6 where He points out *"whom the Lord loves, He chastens and scourges every son whom He receives."* However, the Lord will not abandon them if they will open the door and let Him come in and be the **head of the church**. He is standing at the door and knocking. He extends to them the **promise** that if they will **open the door to Him**, He will come in and fellowship with them by dining with them. The one who is the *"way, the truth and the life"* stands ready to heal their **blindness** and **lethargy** so they can be an effective witness for the Lord

The Meaning of It All

Most Biblical scholars who believe the Scripture also affirm that we are living in the **Laodicean period** or the **final period** of history. There are a few bright spots in church life but the picture, generally, is dismal. Some of the churches that are "growing" have been cult-like about a pastor or an idea. The only measuring stick seems to be the matter of whether or not the church is "growing."

If a church can summon a crowd together they are called "successful" but we must remember that even the mafia can draw a crowd. Let us remember that it takes more than a rock band and a "swinging preacher" to plant and build a real **New Testament church**.

Let us remember, however, that many in the contemporary church are earnest and sincere about their faith in Jesus Christ and the proclamation of His Gospel. Christians should be very slow to condemn the contemporary church until they see clearly what kind of fruit it bears and a few "bad apples" should not turn young people away from real, genuine, Gospel proclaiming churches that will help them to **grow in the faith** of the Lord Jesus Christ. Many churches that are quite **traditional** in their worship forms and their music are still **faithful** to the **Scriptures** and in the **proclamation of the Gospel**. They will love you and provide the facilities and dedicated leadership that will lead you and your children to **grow** in the **grace** and **knowledge** of the Lord and Savior Jesus Christ.

The New Testament Church

In the New Testament, the church is compared to a bride and it is the **Bride of Christ**. This symbolism first appears in John 3: 29 when John the Baptist teaches that Jesus is the **Bridegroom** and He is simply **the friend** of the Bridegroom. In Ephesians 5, Paul compares the relationship between the church and Christ to marriage. As he closes out that passage he says, *"This is a great mystery, but I speak concerning **Christ** and the **church**."* (Ephesians 5: 32) In the Revelation, John uses that same symbolism. He writes to a church in Asia that is led by Gaius in the Letter of III John. While he **commends** Gaius for his Godly leadership he **condemns** Diotrephes who is resisting the missionaries bringing the Gospel and has even refused a letter from John. In the Revelation, John uses the term "**bride**" four times in reference to the church and there are seventeen references to the church. As John closes out the Revelation, he speaks of the bride again, as he says, "*... the **Spirit** and the **Bride** say '**come**'! Let him who thirsts **come**, and whoever **desires**, let him take the water of life freely.*" (Revelation 22: 17) Of course, the work of the **Spirit** is to **convict** the lost person of his need for Christ and (His Bride); the *church* is that institution that invites that person into the family of God. Both the **Spirit** and the **Bride** are to say, "*come.*" Anyone who desires salvation through Jesus Christ may come

John's Pastorate

As pointed out earlier, John pastored the Church at Ephesus for about 20 years but he faced many adversaries there. Paul had established the church. During Paul's final conversation with the Elders of the Ephesian church at Miletus, he talked about how he served the church with many **tears** and **trials** due to the plotting of the Jews. Paul warns them to take heed to themselves and to all the flock over which the **Holy Spirit** has made them **overseers**. They are to **shepherd** the church of God that He purchased with His own blood. He warned them that **savage wolves** would come among them, and **not spare the flock**. He even warned them that some of the men in their own company would rise up and speak perverse things to **draw away disciples after themselves**. He commanded the church elders to **watch** and **be alert** to any problem in the church. With this warning of troubling things they would face in the future he gives them a final charge and sails away to see them no more. It was, of course, John who served as pastor during those troubling times that Paul had prophesied but it is clear that John **believed in the church** and that it was the **body of Christ**.

Today

Yes, the church **is** ministering in **critical days** among great opposition and persecution. Sometimes charlatans use the name of the church for their own vested interests. Let us remember that the church is made up of **imperfect** people. They are **sinners saved by grace**. Sometimes men who come to the church endure great struggles in breaking with the things in their past lives that have dragged them down. The church may not be a **perfect instrument** but it is the instrument of **Christ** for which He **died** as Paul points out in Ephesians 5. If everyone in the church was required to be perfect, not one of us would qualify for membership but it is still the body of Christ. It is in that fellowship and teaching of the church that we grow in grace and knowledge of our Lord and Savior Jesus Christ (II Peter 3: 18). The church is still vital. Sometimes the believer must search diligently to find a church that is true to the Scripture and true to the Spirit of Jesus Christ but they are out there and every believer should search for such a church **until he finds it**. Let there **be no doubt** that the great Apostle John **believed in the church** because it was the body of Christ and he spent most of his life in **service** and **loyalty** to the **church**. Likewise, the inspired words of Paul charge us to " *...consider one another in order to stir up love and good works* **not forsaking the assembling of ourselves together** *as is the manner of some, but exhorting one another so much the more as you see* **the Day** *approaching."* (Hebrews 10: 24-25)

The church is an imperfect vessel ministering to imperfect people while existing in a fallen world but it is still the **body and bride** of Christ that He loved and gave Himself for it to be the incubator and brooder that brings the lost to Christ and leads them to grow in grace until they receive their glorified bodies.

Chapter Five
Is There Really a Resurrection and Judgment?

Young adults are also asking whether there really is a day of Resurrection and Judgment. They deserve an answer to this searching question. Again, we look to the writings of the great Apostle John as he faithfully recorded the teachings of Jesus Himself concerning this vital subject. In the fifth chapter of John's gospel, He reveals a blessed truth to us when he establishes the fact that the Heavenly Father has committed all judgments to the Son (John 5: 22) and that men should honor the Son just as they honor the Father. It is impossible to honor the Father if we do not honor the Son. Then, he gives us that wonderfully assuring truth that those who believe in the Son will have everlasting life and shall never come into condemnation but have passed from **death** unto **life**. It is clear that we have eternal life only through Jesus Christ. It does not come any other way (John 5: 24). After establishing the fact that He is a part of the Godhead, Jesus says, *"Most assuredly, I say to you, the hour is coming and now is when the dead will **hear** the voice of the Son of God and those who **hear** will live. For as the Father has life in Himself, so He has granted the Son to have life in Himself, and this has given Him authority to execute judgment also, because He is the Son of man. Do not marvel at this for the hour is coming in which all who are in the graves will hear His voice and come forth – those who have done good, to the resurrection of life and those who have done evil to the resurrection of condemnation." (John 5: 25-29)*

The Trinity

Jesus asserts here that He is a part of the Trinity (God the Father, God the Son and God the Holy Spirit) and that all power for judgment has been delivered into His hands. There will be a time when everyone will be resurrected from the dead. The seas will give up the dead that are in them. The graves will give up the dead that are in them. Everyone will be judged. Those who have done good will rise to the resurrection of **life** and those who have done evil to the resurrection of **condemnation**. The term "judgment" in this passage comes from the Greek root word krisis (κρισις). It means, "to separate out and render a decision." The word is used forensically and denotes a process of investigation and the act of distinguishing between good and evil. It also means to arrive at a just decision and to assign a verdict. It has the connotation of judicial authority. When Paul speaks of the Judgment in Romans 2: 5 he uses the term dikaiokrisia (δικαιοκρισια) which is translated "righteous judgment." In the course of the world, men are sometimes falsely accused and wrongly judged and sentenced but that will never happen with God because God's judgments are always **righteous judgments**. In this life, men often pass wrongful judgments and develop misplaced attitudes about us but that will never happen when we stand before God. There will be no clever lawyers to sway the course of justice because God the Son (Jesus Christ) knows the truth and we will be judged in truth. His judgment will be tempered with mercy that came from the cross of Christ to those who believe.

The Resurrection day will be a **day of joy** and happiness for those who **know Christ** and have been redeemed by His shed blood at Calvary. To those who do not know Christ and have never embraced Him as their personal savior, it will be the most horrible day of their memory and they will live in horrible torment forever.

Conditions of Judgment

There is a corresponding passage in Matthew 25: 31 – 46. In this passage, Jesus sets the **conditions** of the Judgment. The Son of Man will come with His holy angels and He will sit on the **throne of His glory**. He compares His Judgment there with the separating of sheep from goats. This is a declaration of absolute honesty and fairness. No one can be mistaken about which is a sheep and which is a goat. Many refer to this as the "sheep and goat judgment." He will place the sheep on His right hand and the goats on His left. Then, Jesus will say to those on His right hand, *"Come, ye blessed of My Father, inherit the kingdom prepared for you from the foundation of the world."* In the following verses, Jesus makes it clear that they belong to Him, the great shepherd, because of their ministry in His name but the righteous did not realize many of the things that they did were a **ministry** for the **Lord**. In verse 26, they inquired of Him as to when they had done those great ministries in His name (verses 38 – 39). The answer of the King will be, *"Inasmuch as ye did it to one of the least of these my brethren, ye did it unto Me."*

The Wicked

Then He will say to those on His left hand, *"Depart from me, ye cursed, into everlasting fire prepared for the Devil and his angels."* They have exhibited no responsibility for their witness and service to Jesus Christ. They challenged the Lord's judgment. They began to ask when they were guilty of not serving Him (verse 44). His answer to them will be, *"...inasmuch as ye did not do it unto one of the least of these, ye did not do it to me."* (Verse 45) Jesus makes it plain that those on His left whom He compares to goats will *"go away into everlasting punishment but the righteous into eternal life."*

Many times Christians are discouraged and, sometimes, even intimidated when the world refers to them as "right wingers." If the world wants to give you that title, embrace it with gladness because Jesus makes it clear that those on **His right hand** are those who will be received into a blessed relationship for eternity with the Father, the Son, and the Holy Spirit. In fact, in Ecclesiastes 10: 2 – 3 the preacher says, *"A wise man's heart is at his right hand, but a fool's heart at His left. Even when a fool walks along the way, he lacks wisdom and he shows everyone that he is a fool."* The believer in Christ should never shy away from being at the **right hand of God.**

Job's Testimony

The resurrection from the grave is not something that popped up late in the Bible. Most scholars agree that the book of Job is the oldest book of the Bible. In Job 14: 14 he poses the question: *"If a man dies, shall he live again?"* The question is answered in Chapter 19 when he said: *"For I know that my redeemer lives, and he shall stand at last on the earth, and after my skin is destroyed, this I know, in my flesh I shall see God, whom I shall see for myself and my eyes shall behold and not another. How my heart yearned within me! If you should say, how shall we persecute him? Since the root of the matter is found in me, be afraid of the sword for yourselves; for wrath brings the **punishment** of the sword that ye may know that there is a **judgment**."* (Job 19: 25 – 29) The resurrection is one of the basic beliefs of the Christian faith. In prayer, King David spoke of his belief in the resurrection when he said, *"I will see your face in righteousness; I shall be satisfied **when I awake in your likeness**."* It was Isaiah who spoke of his yearning when he said, *"Your dead shall live; together with my dead body they shall arise. Awake and sing, ye who dwell in dust; for your dew is like the dew of herbs, and the earth shall **cast out** the dead."* (Isaiah 26: 19) The prophet Daniel spoke of his belief in the resurrection when he said, *"And many of those who sleep in the dust of the earth shall awake, some to everlasting life, some to shame and everlasting contempt."* (Daniel 12: 2) Daniel began to prophesy almost 600 years before Christ, but Jesus Himself confirmed what Daniel said!

Other Records

However, the writings of John that we have considered are not the only ones that record Jesus' teaching concerning the resurrection. In Matthew 22: 29 – 32 we have the record of Jesus upbraiding the Sadducees because they denied the resurrection and he made it clear that there is a resurrection. That occasion is reported in all three of the synoptic gospels (See Mark 12: 24 – 27; Luke 20: 34 – 38).

In addition to the John 5 passage, Jesus assured those who believed in Him that they would be raised from the dead. In that famous passage with which Pastors comfort the bereaved, Jesus said, *"I am the resurrection and the life, he who believes in Me though he may die, he shall live."* (John 11: 25) He emphasized His power to raise the dead again in John 6: 39 – 40 when he said, *"This is the will of the Father who sent me, that of all He has given me I should lose nothing, but should raise it up at the last day. And this is the will of Him who sent me, that everyone who sees the Son and believes in Him may have everlasting life; and I will raise him up at the last day."* The resurrection theme is repeated again in Acts 2, 4, 17, 23, 24 and 26.

Paul and the Resurrection

Of course, then, there is that powerful presentation in I Corinthians 15 where Paul so persuasively presents the fact of the resurrection in the first eleven verses. In reminding the

Corinthians that some of those at Corinth had succumbed to some kind of Saduceean influence and were declaring that there was no resurrection of the dead (verse 12). Paul reminded them that not only had all the apostles, including him, witnessed the Lord after the resurrection but also over 500 people at one time had witnessed the resurrected Christ. He declared to them that if Christ is not risen, then their preaching and faith is all in vain and they would be found false witnesses. He also reminded them that if Christ were not risen then they were yet in their sins and that if man has hope in this life only, he will be of *"all men most pitiable."* (Verse 19) In verses 20 – 26 Paul presents the order of resurrection. To those at Corinth who were confused about the resurrection body Paul sets their minds at ease when he compares the resurrection to a seed planted. The seed that is produced is not the same one that is planted but the fruit of that seed planted will be new seed. In the same way, we will be raised in a new body but just as the seed produced is very much like the seed planted, our resurrection body will be very much like the body that was planted. We shall have a new but recognizable body. That body that was buried may have been wracked with cancer or diabetes or Alzheimer disease. It may have been crippled by polio, arthritis, war or stroke but it will be *"raised in incorruption."* (I Corinthians 15: 42) Our heavenly bodies will be whole and free from those things that have harmed our bodies in this life because these things will have passed away. *"And God will wipe away every tear from their eyes; there shall be no more death, nor sorrow, nor crying; and there shall be no more pain, for the former things have passed away."* (Revelation 21: 4)

What Shall We Know?

Will we know our friends and loved ones in heaven? The Scriptures say, "Yes." I Corinthians 13:12 makes that clear. *"For now we see in a mirror, dimly, but then face to face. Now I know in part, but then I shall know just as I also am known."* The Apostle Paul asserts emphatically that in the resurrection we will have a new and glorified body. His teaching was in perfect harmony with John who made it clear that we would have a body like that of the Lord (I John 3: 2). He further explains to them that those who are alive when Christ returns will be changed in a moment or in the twinkling of an eye at the last trumpet and that the dead in Christ will be raised incorruptible. Those who are remaining and alive will be changed into their eternal bodies. The corruptible will put on incorruption and the mortal will put on immortality which means that **"death is swallowed up in victory."** He ended the chapter by calling upon the people at Corinth to be *"steadfast, immovable, always abounding in the work of the Lord, knowing that your labor is not in vain in the Lord."* (I Corinthians 15: 58)

The Issues of the Judgment

Following the resurrection, there will be judgment. Scholars agree that those who are brought to the Great White Throne Judgment are the wicked dead and the wicked that are alive who have rejected Christ. Some refer to that as the Judgment of Nations as pointed out earlier. The judgment of Matthew 25 is known as the Sheep and Goat Judgment. Of course, there are times when God judges nations and people on this earth but His judgment will always be fair and done according to truth (Romans 2: 2). There are temporal judgments. God judged Lucifer at one point (II Peter 2: 4; Jude 6). The Genesis' flood was an act of God's judgment (Genesis 6: 7). He judged Nimrod and his followers at the Tower of Babel (Genesis 11: 1 – 9). He judged Israel at one time by sending her into captivity (II Kings 25: 1 – 12). Shortly after Pentecost, God judged the church when Ananias and Sapphira lied to the Holy Spirit of God (Acts 5: 1 - 11). The wrath of God is often revealed against ungodliness and unrighteousness (Romans 1: 18). The judgments of God on this earth are not the final judgment. In the John 5 passage that we have considered, Jesus assured the world of His **authority to judge**. Believers will be judged at the Bema or the "judgment seat of Christ" (II Corinthians 5: 10). In that judgment, believers will be rewarded for the deeds that they have done while in their earthly bodies. They will be judged according to the kind of deeds that they have performed, whether they be good or bad (II Corinthians 5: 10). At that judgment, Christians will face their service record for Christ whether they were known for good deeds or bad deeds. In the closing verse of the chapter Paul unleashes that wonderful claim in his recognition that, *"He made him who knew no sin to be sin for us, that we might become the righteousness of God in Him."* (Verse 21)

Believer's Judgment

Every believer looks forward to that glorified body that John speaks of which we have discussed earlier. There will be a time when believers who have been unfaithful will stand before the judgment seat of Christ and have their works examined. It will be a testing as of by fire. For those whose work stands the testing at the judgment seat of Chris they will receive rewards. Those who have been unfaithful will see their works destroyed as if by fire and they will suffer loss of their work but their soul will be saved *"yet so as through fire."* (I Corinthians 3: 14) In the next verse, Paul admonishes them to remember that their bodies are the temple of God. That is the reason that Christians should never defile their bodies. They are warned against church partisanship in the closing verses of the chapter because they, *"are Christ's"* and *"Christ is God's."* (Verses 22 & 23)

Loss of Fellowship with God

We see moreover, that the issues of the Judgment for the wicked means to lose all hope and fellowship with God in eternity and to be confined to an eternal Hell. That is the most horrible thing that any individual can imagine. The most sinful and condemning thing that any person can do is to reject the Son of God. John faithfully quotes Jesus in John 3: 18 when he said, *"He who believes in Him is not condemned; but he who **does not believe** is condemned already, **because he has not believed in the name of the only begotten Son of God.**"* The sin of unbelief is the most insulting and hurtful thing against the heart of God and the love of God that any individual can commit because God sent His only Son that *"whosoever believes in Him should not perish but have everlasting life."* (John 3: 16) Nothing is more offensive to God the Father or the Son than to reject God's love after God sent His only Son to redeem us.

These Scriptures behoove every Christian to live uprightly and honestly before God. Those Christians who are good stewards and who serve faithfully in the work of the Kingdom will find blessed rewards at the judgment seat of Christ. That Christian who is unfaithful and continues to toy with the world will be **saved as by fire** as we have pointed out earlier but their works will be burned up because they were performed with the wrong motivation.

Assurance of Christ

It is the assurance of Christ, Himself, when He promised that He will *"come again and receive you to Myself; that where I am, there you may be also."* (John 14: 3) For now, Christ is preparing a place for all believers in the Heavenly City that John writes about in Revelation 21. When He returns, we will be caught up with Him in the air and so shall we ever be with the Lord (I Thessalonians

4: 17 – 18). Whatever else Heaven may be, it means that we will have fellowship with the One who died for us to redeem us from sin and reconcile us to God. For anyone to deny that there will be a resurrection and a judgment would be to strike at the very character of God because He demands, and His holiness must assure, that justice is done fairly and righteously. **Yes, His character demands it.** It behooves every person on earth to be ready for our Lord's return and the judgment that is to follow.

About Those Who Have Never Heard

What about those who have never heard the Gospel? How will they be judged in the judgment? In the very first chapter of John's Gospel, as he describes Jesus' mission in the world, he states that Jesus was the *"true light which gives light to **every man** who comes into the world."* (John 1: 9) The message of that passage is that everyone who comes into the world has **some light** even though he may not have heard the complete Gospel. There is an intuitive knowledge of what is right and wrong. For instance, even in pagan lands men know that it is wrong to kill. They know that it is wrong to lie. They know it is wrong to steal and to covet. They know that it is wrong to commit adultery. We find an example of this when Paul and Barnabas were at Lystra. Paul saw a man who was a cripple from birth. Paul sensed that he had faith to be healed. Paul commanded the man to stand on his feet and he did. Of course, Paul had healed him in the name of Jesus but there were many pagans living in Lystra. They worshipped strange gods. When they saw what Paul and Barnabas had done, they had wanted to call Barnabas, Zeus, or Jupiter and they wanted to call Paul, Hermes, or Mercury. When a priest of the Temple of Zeus heard of it he brought oxen and garlands to the gates in order to make sacrifice with the multitudes. When Paul and Barnabas heard about this, they were so upset that they tore their clothes and ran among the multitude crying out, *"Men, why are you doing these things? We also are men with the same nature as you, and preach to you that you should turn from these vain things to the living God, who made the Heaven, the Earth, the Sea and all things that are in them, who in bygone generations allowed all nations to walk in their own ways."* Then, Luke, the writer of Acts, gives the decisive factor. He quoted Paul who said, *"Nevertheless He did not leave Himself without witness, in that He did good, gave us rain from Heaven and fruitful seasons, filling our hearts with food and gladness."* (Acts 14: 15 – 17)

Lesson of Lystra

The great lesson here is, as pointed out in Chapter Two, that the people of Lystra could look at the world around them and see the good things that God had done by providing fruitful seasons and rain from heaven so that the people could live. Paul made it clear that even the pagans of Lystra were not left **without witness** and no man on the face of the earth is **totally without witness about the living God**. Sometimes pagan people understand that there is something beyond themselves and they worship things of nature such as the sun or the moon. However, Christians never worship nature but we worship the **God of nature**.

When the early settlers came to America they found Indians who had never heard the Gospel but even they recognized that there was a "great Spirit" in the world that controlled the world. Therefore, we see that no man is totally without light. It is **true** as John said that the **Light** provides **light** to **every man** who comes into the world. (See John 1:9) It is also true that all of those pagan civilizations had the opportunity to know God but they refused to glorify Him as God. They turned away from God. Professing to be "wise," they turned to foolish things such as worshipping images of humans and beasts. (Romans 1: 18-23) That is the reason Paul says they are "**without excuse**"! That is because all mankind came from the **same ancestry**! All mankind had the opportunity to **know God**!

What Say The Scriptures?

In John 9: 41 Jesus confronts the matter. Jesus had healed a blind man. When the blind man told the Pharisees that Jesus had healed his sight, they disputed his claim and cast him out (John 9:34). When Jesus saw him again he asked, "*Do you believe in the Son of God?*" When the formerly blind man asked, "*Who is he, Lord, that I may believe in Him?*" Jesus' answer to him was, "*You have both seen Him and it is He who is talking to you.*" (Verse 37) The man's answer was, "*Lord, I believe!*" and he worshipped the Lord.

At that point Jesus said, "*For judgment I have come into this world that those who do not see may see and that those who see may be made blind.*" (Verse 39)

The Pharisees who were with Him heard these words and they lashed out at Jesus saying, "*Are we blind also?*" (Verse 40) It was then that Jesus said to them, "*If you were blind, you would have no sin; but now you say, 'We see.' Therefore, your sin remains.*" (Verse 41) Again, we see that men will be judged based on the **light against which they have sinned**!

In John 15: 22 Jesus comes over that same teaching again. Jesus had warned his disciples that they would be persecuted by the world. He warned them that the world would love its' own but because they were not of the world and He had chosen them out of the world, then the world would hate them (verses 18 – 19). Jesus also warned them that the servant is not greater than his master and that if they, of the world, were willing to persecute

Jesus they would also persecute His followers. Then He said, "*If I had not come and spoken to them, they would have no sin but now they have no excuse for their sin.*" (Verse 22) He re-emphasizes it in verse 24 when He said, "*If I had not done among them the works that no one else did, they would have no sin; but now they have seen and also **hated both Me and My Father.**"* (Verse 24) The truth of God is inescapable here. They will be judged because they have had opportunity to know the truth and they rejected it. They, too, will be judged **according to the light against which they sinned**.

The Luke 12: 47 – 48 passage that we have quoted earlier in another setting is also appropriate here. The servant who knew his master's will and did not according to his will, is to be punished more severely than the servant who did not know his master's will even though he had committed things worthy of stripes but he will be punished less severely than the person who has committed an offense against his master even though he knew the master's will. Again, the judgment meted out is based on the **light and knowledge against which he sinned**.

When Jesus was hanging on the cross, the first thing He did was to pray, "*Father, forgive them for they do not **know what they do.**"* (Luke 22: 34) Those who were crucifying Jesus were doing the most heinous thing that any man could have ever done and yet Jesus asked the Father to forgive them. What was the basis upon which Jesus asked the Father to forgive them? It was because they **did not know** what they did. Again, the criteria were the **light and knowledge against which they sinned.**

What Does This Mean to Us?

To those who have heard the Gospel repeatedly and yet have rejected that Gospel, I must say to them that they are guiltier and more wicked than were the people of Sodom. In Matthew 11: 24

187

Jesus was upbraiding cities like Capernaum where Jesus had taught in their synagogue. It was near Capernaum that Jesus fed the 5,000. It was not far from Capernaum that He fed the 4,000. It was near Capernaum that He walked on the water. Jesus made it clear to them that if He had done the same great works in the City of Sodom that He had done among them, the people of Sodom would have repented. Nevertheless, He made it clear that it would be **more tolerable** in the judgment for the wicked city of Sodom than for those people in Galilee who had witnessed His mighty works and heard His teachings; yet they **rejected** them. **Sodom** – think of that – it was a city that was so wicked it became the name of the most revolting crime that man can think of. The American legal system, for many years, called that crime **sodomy** but yet God could look on Sodom with more comfort than He could look upon people who had heard the Gospel and seen the great works of Jesus but who rejected them. Look upon the Hindu Juggernaut with its' worshippers throwing themselves under its wheels to be crushed to death, or that despairing young mother who sacrifices her baby in the mouth of a crocodile at the "sacred" River Ganges. Look at the natives in the Belgian Congo or the Aborigines in the desolate places of Australia. They may have strange and pagan customs but their customs will not offend God as much as the indifference of the American who breezes by the House of God on the Lord's Day travelling toward the Devil's playground looking for the illusive satisfaction everywhere but in the House of God. The Spiritism of the natives in the Amazon regions is not as offensive to God as that person who has heard the Gospel thousands of times, by radio, from the pulpit, by television, by internet and many other ways and yet has rejected Jesus. In all of these, we see that inexorable law of God who is faithful, fair, and just in His judgments and always, He judges us according to the **light against which we sin**

About Children

Often there are people who worry about children who die before they are old enough to understand the Gospel. We do not ever have to be afraid that we love those children more than God loves them and we can comfortably leave them in the hands of God because He is righteous and just. We can always trust God to be merciful, compassionate, and just.

Conclusion

We believe that we have produced adequate evidence in this chapter that there really is a resurrection and a judgment. We have used the highest and most authoritative sources known to man in this presentation. We believe that we have presented these universal truths to the satisfaction of any reasonable mind; but you still must walk by **faith**. **Faith is the bedrock of Christianity**. In fact, faith was the very theme of Jesus' ministry. In the Sermon on the Mount Jesus said, *"Now if God so clothed the grass of the field which today is, and tomorrow is thrown into the oven, will He not much more clothe you, Oh ye of little **faith**."* (Matthew 6: 30) He promised His followers that if they would have the **faith** of a grain of mustard seed, they could move mountains (Matthew 17: 20). In Luke 17: 5, we have the record of the disciples asking the Lord to *"increase our **faith**."* In Acts 26: 18, we are taught that we are sanctified by faith. In Hebrews 11: 6, we are told *"without **faith** it is impossible to please Him, for he who comes to God must believe that He is, and that He is the rewarder of those who diligently seek Him."* In Romans 10: 17 we are told that *"**faith** comes by hearing and hearing by the **Word of God**."* In Ephesians 2: 8, we are taught that *"by grace you have been saved through **faith**, and that not of yourselves; it is the gift of God."* In I John 1: 9 John speaks of the process of salvation as he says, *"If we* *confess our sins He is **faithful** and just to forgive us our sins and to cleanse from all unrighteousness."* As John was explaining how believers gain victory over the world he said, *"This is the victory that has overcome the world - our **faith**."* (I John 5: 4) Young adults who would live victorious Christian lives would be wise to learn early the admonition of Paul who said, *"We walk by **faith**, not by sight."* (I Corinthians 5: 7) As we walk by **faith**, these truths that we have discussed will become more and more **evident**.

Chapter Six
Is There Really a
Heaven and Hell?

The first mention of Heaven in the Bible is in the first verse of the first chapter when the Scripture says, *"In the beginning God created the heavens and the earth."* This fact is affirmed by John in the first chapter of his Gospel where he declares that Jesus (the Word) was with God and the **Word was God**. He is declaring that God and Christ are **one** and that Christ was right there in the beginning. In John 1: 3, he declares that *"**all things were made through Him**, and without Him **nothing** was **made** that was made."* In John 3: 13 he quotes the pronouncement of Jesus when he said, *"**No one has ascended unto heaven but He who came down from heaven, that is the Son of Man who is in heaven.**"*

Mythology

The world has always **concocted false gods**. As we pointed out earlier, John was pastor of the church at Ephesus, which was right in the midst of Greek culture. The greatest tumult that the city had ever seen was probably the riot that was caused by the Silversmiths when Paul was preaching there and multitudes were turning to Christ. So great was the conversion of the pagans to Christianity that the Silversmiths started a riot because they made their living by making shrines to the Goddess Diana as was discussed earlier. They feared that so many turning to Christ would ruin their business. The world will usually react viciously if they think devotion to God will hurt their pocketbooks. There were numerous sordid stories about gods and goddesses in the

Greek culture. There were all kinds of mythological stories floating around the Greek world about such individuals as Homer or Virgil who travelled the earth finding mythical figures that they believed affected the destinies of man. Even the Gnostics concocted mythological explanations of an alien messenger visiting the Cosmos. There were stories about mythical figures like Sophia who perverted natural relationships and caused the creation of this sub-world in which we live. Jesus clarifies it all. He assures the world that no mortal man has ever ascended to Heaven except the "*Son of Man*" who came down from the Father. The term "*Son of Man*" is a reference to Daniel 7: 13-14 where the **Son of Man** is used in reference to the **second person of the Trinity** who was given dominion, glory and a kingdom that all languages and people should serve Him and that His dominion would be everlasting and His kingdom would not pass away. In this passage, God the Father is presented as the "*Ancient of Days.*" When Jesus referred to Himself as the "*Son of Man,*" He was declaring that He was the **fulfillment** of that prophecy from the book of Daniel. Christians should never allow themselves to be deceived by liberal theologians who try to persuade them that Christianity grew out of pagan mythology. It has never been based on the idea that some mortal became so great and powerful that he or she **ascended to the heavens** and became a god. That sort of thing has no basis whatever in factual history. John makes it clear from the teachings of Jesus Himself that we are redeemed only by the **Son of God** who **came down from Heaven.**

The Parthenon, one of the most perfect buildings ever built on earth was built to the goddess Athena. Her image was garnished with ivory and precious stones but in the end, she was made by the hands of men out of nothing more than earthly material and was totally **without life!** Jesus actually lived, died, **rose again** and is alive forever more! He is now making intercession **for us!** (Hebrews 7:25 & Romans 8:34)

Heaven

John's declaration of Heaven is affirmed again in I John 5: 7 where He also stresses the Trinity of God the **Father**, God the **Son**, and God the **Holy Spirit**. He declares that these three are one.

The Greek word that is translated *"Heaven"* is ouranos (ουρανος). It is from here that the Son of God descended to become incarnate in the flesh. It literally refers to the **eternal dwelling place of God**. John the Baptist bears similar witness to the truth that Jesus descended from Heaven to become incarnate in the flesh and is above all. John again quotes Jesus in his great "Bread of Life" discourse when Jesus said, *"...I have **come down from heaven** not to do my own will, but the will of Him who sent Me."* There are many other references in the New Testament teachings of Jesus about Heaven.

Moreover, John faithfully records the pronouncement of Jesus as to who will occupy the Heavenly Kingdom when He said, *"....the hour is coming in which all who are in the graves will hear His voice and come forth – those who have done good to the **resurrection of life**, and those who have done evil, to the **resurrection of condemnation**."* (John 5: 38 – 39) Jesus makes it clear in this passage that our assignment to Heaven is not without regard to the way we have lived our lives on earth. When the voice of the Lord is heard by those who have gone before at the time of resurrection, those who have *"**done good**"* will be raised to eternal life or the *"resurrection of life"* and those who have *"**done evil"*** will be raised to the resurrection of condemnation or, as the King James puts it, *"**damnation**."* This Scripture should be a warning to those who think that simply joining a church or signing a card will prepare them for Heaven. Heaven is a **prepared place for prepared people**. The person who becomes a nominal Christian but who has no interest in **living the Christian life** may well be disappointed on the Day of Judgment when the dead shall be brought forth

Heaven Is a Place

In the fourteenth chapter of John, he again presents our Lord's teachings about Heaven. He faithfully quotes the words of Jesus who said, *"In my Father's House are many mansions; if it were not so, I would have told you. I go to prepare a **place** for you. And if I go and prepare a place for you, I will come again and **receive you unto myself**; that **where I am there you may be also**. And whither I go you know and the way you know."* (John 14: 2-4) These three beautiful verses are packed with Divine **truth!** The term, *"my Father's House"* is translated from the Greek word *oikos* (οικος). In this case, it is used to denote the whole estate. For instance, the Bible tells us that Joseph was of the *"**house and lineage of David**."* (Luke 2: 4) The angel announced to Mary that she would bear a son who would, *"reign over the **house of Jacob** forever and of His kingdom there will be no end."* (Luke 1: 33) Jesus is saying that our Father's House includes everything that belongs to the Father, not just a structure where beings live and sleep. He is referring to our Father who created the heavens and the earth (Genesis 1: 1). He is the Father who owns the *"cattle on a thousand hills."* (Psalm 50: 10) Every one of us who are saved has a place in the Father's **household** or **estate**.

Again, John states that our Father's House has many **mansions**. This word is translated from the word *uonai* (υοναι). It means an abode or a dwelling place. Jesus makes it clear that He will go to prepare a **place** for us so we understand that Heaven is **not a state of being but a place**.

Our Glorified Bodies

In I John 3: 2 John tells us what our heavenly bodies will be like when he says, "Beloved now are we children of God; and it has not yet been revealed what we shall be, but we know that when He is revealed, **we shall be like Him**, for we shall see Him as He is." This tells us that in our resurrection body, we will be like Christ or **we** will have a **body** like **His body**. John readily states that, while we know that we are children of God we do not know exactly what our bodies will be like except that we know that they will be like the body of Jesus. What was Jesus' resurrection body like? In His **resurrection body**, Jesus passed through closed doors. On the evening of the resurrection Jesus came and stood in the midst of the disciples even though the doors were shut (John 20: 19). He showed them His hands and His side and the disciples were glad. In His resurrection body, He also ate food. In the Upper Room where the Disciples were gathered He ate a piece of broiled fish and a honeycomb (Luke 24: 42). We do not understand that kind of body as John confessed he did not understand it. However, we know that it is the kind of body that we will have because that is the **kind of body Jesus had after His resurrection**.

The Appearance of Heaven

The Lord, through the Apostle John, gives us a more detailed account concerning the appearance of Heaven than any other writer of Scripture. Not only does the Scripture assure us that Jesus has gone to prepare a **place** for us; but it is a place that is located in a new heaven and a new earth (Revelation 21: 1). The old heaven and earth will pass away.

It is a place where God will *"tabernacle"* with men. The word tabernacle here is translated from the Greek word *skene* (σκενέ). The tabernacle in the wilderness was referred to as the *"tent of meeting."* (Acts 7: 44-50) The word literally means, "to pitch a tent." It indicates close relationships. God will "pitch His tent" **with us**. That is the way John describes the coming of Jesus. In John 1: 14 the term *"dwelt among us"* is referring to a tabernacle. Jesus, in other words, came to "pitch His tent" with us. It is translated that He *"came to dwell among us."* The tabernacle in the wilderness was a place where the Israelites went to commune with God. The word is used in II Corinthians 5: 1. This Scripture refers to our earthly bodies as a "tabernacle" or a "tent" that is temporary. However, we will put off this earthly tabernacle in Heaven and receive a *"**building** from **God**, a house not made with hands, **eternal** in the heavens."* (II Corinthians 5: 1-8) This tells us that we will have **intimate fellowship** with God and the **government** of **Heaven** will be a pure government lead by a loving, eternal God and His Son Jesus Christ where there will be no more corruption, falsehoods, and hurt such as we see from corrupt governments on earth. We will see Him **face to face** and **know** as we are **known** (I Corinthians 13: 12).

Its Beauty

Heaven is a place of unimaginable beauty. Not only is it a place of beautiful mansions in which the redeemed will dwell, but it is a place of beauty that is beyond the power of our tongues to describe. The same God who created the moon and the stars; the Grand Canyon and the redwood forest; the painted deserts of the southwest that bloom like the Rose of Sharon in the Spring. The same God who created the beautiful red Robins, the Bluebirds who remain together as a family throughout their lives, the Goldfinches, the beautiful Cardinals, the Pheasants and the Canaries as well as the Deer and the Antelope, **also created Heaven**. The earth with its' beautiful velvet carpets of green in the Springtime, its' flaming colors of Fall in the Blue Ridge Mountains, also created Heaven. **Heaven is His masterpiece!** John describes Heaven in earthly terms as being like " *... jasper; and the city was pure gold, like clear glass."* (Revelation 21: 18) He describes the city as being pure gold with foundations garnished with jasper, sapphire, chalcedony, emerald, sardius, chrysolite, beryl, topaz, chrysoprase, jacinth, and amethyst. He describes the gates as being made of pure pearl. Unlike the streets of this earth, the streets of Heaven are pure gold that is so highly refined that it is like clear glass, which means that there were no impurities in it whatever. In the Heavenly city, everything will be beautiful. There will be no blight as we face in cities on this earth. Even the **foundation stones** are garnished with beautiful gems.

It is a spacious place (Revelation 21:15-16). We will never hear of inner city overcrowding as we hear on earth today. The new heavenly city will be 1,500 miles long, 1,500 miles wide and 1,500 miles high. It will be a perfect cube. Earthly beings could never dream of building such a city. That city will be filled with spacious mansions. The walls of the city will be approximately 216 feet thick.

God's Glory

Our heavenly city is lighted by the very **glory of God**. There will be no need for the sun or the moon in the heavenly city. There will be no part of it that will be poorly lit. God will be among us and **be our God** and we will **be His people**. We shall live in the light of His glory (verse 23). Throughout the Bible, light has symbolized the presence of God. In the creation account of Genesis 1 God's first movement of development was, *"Let there be light."* Without the sun the world would be a place of darkness and totally uninhabitable. The earth's rivers, its' arteries, would be frozen. Nothing could grow. No photosynthesis could take place. No human life could exist. In John 1: 4, he describes Jesus by saying, *"In Him was life and the life was the **light** of men and the **light shines in darkness** and the darkness did not comprehend it."* John the Baptist freely confessed that he was *"not that **light**, but was sent to **bear witness of that light**."* (Verse 8) In Heaven, we will see the ultimate of that light

A City of Joy

Heaven will be a place of ultimate **joy** and **happiness**. It will be a place of untold satisfaction. Those times of tears come to us on earth. Our little homes that are filled in early years with the happy voices of children and the loving voices of parents finally dwindle away. One by one the occupants pass on in death because it is appointed unto man *"once to die and after that the judgment."* (Hebrews 9: 27 KJV) Someone has reminded us that statistically, ten out of ten people die. Old age and loneliness is a source of sorrow. Sometimes we meet failure and persecution in this life that brings sorrow. Sometimes our children break our hearts but in Heaven we are assured that *"God will wipe away every tear from their eyes and there shall be no more death, nor sorrow, nor crying; and there shall be no more pain, for the former things have passed away."* (Revelation 21: 4) The things of earth that cause all of these things will be gone in Heaven because *"He who sat on the throne said, 'Behold I make all things new;'"* because our Lord is the *"alpha and the omega."* He is the beginning and ending of all things and He will *"give of the fountain of the water of life freely to him who thirsts."* (Revelation 21: 6) This is the fulfillment of the promise of Jesus to the woman at the well when he said, *"Whoever drinks of the water that I shall give him shall never thirst. But the water that I shall give him will become in him a fountain of water springing up into everlasting life..."* (John 4: 14) **What a tremendous fulfillment of our Lord's promise!** Not only will God wipe away all tears but also His promise is that the believer will *"inherit all* *things, and I will be his God and he shall be My son."(*Revelation 21: 7) All of our needs will be satisfied by a Heavenly Father who will have that intimate fellowship with us and provide for every need we have.

A Place of God's Protection

Heaven is a place where the saints will be perfectly safe from the evils that have plagued us in the world. The Lord points out that *"the cowardly, unbelieving, abominable, murderers, sexually immoral, sorcerers, adulterers and all liars will not be in Heaven"* but will occupy a place that He calls the *"lake which burns with fire and brimstone, which is the second death."* (Revelation 21: 8) We will discuss that more later.

The safety of the Heavenly city, where saints will abide, will be protected by angels at the twelve gates of that city. There will be three gates on each side of the city. In this life, we have to take all kinds of measures to protect ourselves and our homes from evil doers. We can even be hurt by people who attack our personal computers in our own homes. People who send their children to school have to worry about sexual predators and assassins. Our own nation of America has been rocked by a terrorist attack that killed almost 3,000 people on 9/11 and continues to threaten. American soldiers have died on foreign soil protecting us from despots who would invade our country and change our way of life. We worry about terrible diseases that can be foisted upon us by evil doers. All of that will be gone in Heaven. There will be no more death or crying. There will be no more sorrow. There will be no more vicious attacks because all of these things will be gone in that Heavenly city where we are totally protected by the great power of God and His holy angels. **No one will be permitted to enter that Heavenly city unless he has been saved through the shed blood of Jesus Christ at Calvary!** There will be no hospitals or funeral homes. There will be no need for prisons or gas chambers or electric chairs or execution gurneys because we will have glorified bodies and only the redeemed shall occupy Heaven.

Because Heaven is a place of God's protection, only those who are prepared for Heaven will be there. The person who came saying "Let me in. I was very useful on earth. I endowed colleges. I built churches. I served on committees in the community. I served on church committees. I was famous for my charities." To those the judge will have to say, "I never knew you." Unless they have been cleansed from sin by the blood of Jesus Christ they cannot enter. We must never give up the clear Biblical teaching of blood redemption at Calvary. Some will say, "Lord, we have eaten and drunk in your presence. You have taught in our streets." However, again, the Lord will say to them, "I never knew you." (Matthew 7: 22-23) The Scripture is clear that not everyone who cries "Lord, Lord" will enter into the Heavenly kingdom.

Heaven Is Open to All

While Heaven is a place of God's protection, it is not a closed society. The great city of God has twelve gates, three on each side of the city. While angels guard the gate, the redeemed of the Lord will be permitted in. All the redeemed will hear the Lord in the Judgment say, *"Come ye blessed of My Father, inherit the kingdom prepared for you from the foundation of the world."* (Matthew 25: 34)

How Do We Get There?

Of course, it is the dream of every believer to go to that wonderful place called Heaven, which, as we have stated, is the dwelling place of God. Again, the great Apostle John records those wonderful words of Jesus in John 3: 16 when Jesus was setting forth His reason for coming to the earth when He said, "... *God so loved the world that He gave His only begotten Son, that **whoever believes in Him** shall not perish but have everlasting life.*" In the following verse, He makes it clear that God had not sent His Son into the world "*to condemn the world, but that the world through Him might be saved.*" John makes it emphatic, by quoting Jesus that the way to Heaven is through the door of salvation. In verse 18 of that chapter He also makes it clear that those who believe in Christ are "*not condemned*" but that those who do not believe are "*condemned already*" simply **because they have not believed**

Reality of Heaven

In that wonderfully moving passage in John 14 when Jesus describes the reality of Heaven and He announced that He is going to prepare a place for His followers, Thomas had a struggle with that promise. It didn't mean that Thomas was an agnostic or that he had the least doubt about who Jesus was but Thomas was an honest man who didn't pretend to understand something if he didn't. He asked, "*Lord, we do not know where you are going, how can we know the way?*" It was then that Jesus gave him that answer that has been heard around the world. It is an answer under whose banner Billy Graham has preached all over the world and under that banner he has seen millions come to know Jesus Christ. What were those powerful moving words that Jesus spoke? Jesus did not scold him for asking the question. He simply said to him, "*I am the way, the truth, and the life. No one comes to the Father except through Me. If you had known Me, you would have known My Father also; and from now on you know Him and have **seen** Him.*" Thomas must have reeled after that answer. Then, however, Phillip had a problem that he revealed when he said, "*Lord, show us the Father, and it is sufficient for us.*"

201

Jesus responded with a soft rebuke when He said, "Have I been with you so long, and yet you have not known Me Phillip? He who has **seen Me** has seen the **Father**, so how can you say, 'show us the Father'?" Jesus then proceeds to explain to him, "I am in the Father and the Father in Me. The words that I speak to you I do not speak on my own authority; but the Father who dwells in Me does the works. Believe Me that I am in the Father and the Father in Me, or else believe Me **for the sake of the works themselves.**" Jesus affirms very forcefully that to see Him was to see the Father because He and the Father are one. He also clarified the reason for miracles. They were done that men might **believe**. Again, there are not many ways to Heaven; there is only **one,** and that is through Jesus Christ.

A Look at the Revelation

As we look in the Revelation following Jesus' explanation to John concerning the city called Heaven, we learn that: "...the nations of those who are **saved** shall walk in its' light, and the kings of the earth shall bring their glory and honor into it." He brings joy to the heart of the believer when He promises, "Its' gates shall not be shut at all by day" (there shall be no night there). Finally, John closes that beautiful chapter of the angel's revelation to him by stating that "There shall by no means enter into it anything that defiles or causes an abomination or a lie, but only those who are written in the lamb's book of life." (Revelation 21: 24 – 27)

This tells us that God keeps books and every one of every age who has been saved has his name written in the Lamb's Book of Life but those who have not chosen the path of salvation are not there. It does not get any more powerful than that! Heaven is a welcoming place for those who have put their faith and trust in Jesus Christ as their Savior and Lord but the only entrance for anyone into the Heavenly City is through Jesus Christ, the Son of God!

Then there are those comforting, beautiful words of Jesus who, after announcing that He would prepare a place for all of us who are believers gave us those touching, moving, promising and beautiful words that "**Where I am there you may be also**." (John 14: 3)

Eternal Hell

The most ill, foreboding and heart-rending words in the English language are those terrible words: "*eternal Hell.*" Yes, there is an eternal Hell. It is not a happy thought. Christians do not enjoy talking about it. Pastors do not enjoy preaching about it. They had rather preach about Heaven or the grace of God or the love of God or Christian discipleship. Eternal Hell is not a pleasant subject but if we are to be faithful to the Scripture and to the teachings of Jesus, we must **tell the whole truth** about an eternal Hell. For the most graphic and detailed description of Hell we turn to John. After Satan makes one last attempt to destroy the people of God, fire comes down from Heaven and devours Satan and his forces. At that point the Devil is cast into a lake of fire and brimstone where the deceiving beast and false prophet dwell (Revelation 20:10).

This is followed by a scene that is referred to as the "Great White Throne" judgment. At that Great White Throne judgment, all the wicked dead are to be assembled both great and small and "*the books are opened.*" Another book that was opened is known as the "*Book of Life.*" Everyone was gathered before the Great White Throne and "*they were judged every man according to their works.*" The Bible makes it unmistakable that "*whosoever was not found written in the Book of Life was cast into the lake of fire.*" (Revelation 20: 11 – 15) This was referred to as the **second** death.

Reigning With Christ

In John's vision, those who had reigned with Christ during the Millennium of 1,000 years were a part of the first resurrection and the Bible makes it clear that *"on such the second death hath no power, but they shall be priests of God and of Christ, and shall reign with Him a thousand years."* (Revelation 20: 4-6) The word John uses for Hell is "hades" (ἄδης). At this point, we must caution about some Bible translations that are available. Some translate the word "Hades" as the grave. That is an incorrect translation. The most outstanding Modern Greek scholars remind us that the term simply refers to the **"realm of the departed dead."** Jesus revealed to John that Hell was a place where there was **fire** and **brimstone**. Jesus, himself, makes that abundantly clear in His account of the rich man and Lazarus found in Luke 16: 19-31. Of the rich man, Jesus said, *"And being in **torments in Hades**, he lifted up his eyes and saw Abraham afar off, and Lazarus in his bosom. Then he cried and said, 'Father Abraham, have mercy on me, and send Lazarus that he may dip the tip of his finger in water and **cool** my tongue; for I am **tormented** in this **flame**."* (Luke 16: 23 – 24) That is the way **Jesus Himself** said it.

The rich man's vision from Hell was that Lazarus was in the presence (bosom) of Abraham and the rich man was in an eternal Hell. He makes it clear that he was **tormented in flames**. Abraham also made it clear to him that there was a great gulf fixed that could never be crossed by people from Hell or from Heaven going into Hell, or going to rescue someone they may know. In verse 25 Abraham reminds the rich man that he had what was considered a good life on earth and Lazarus had a life of suffering and evil. So, it becomes obvious that even in Hell people will carry their **memory** over with them. The rich man **remembered** his five brothers and he desired that Abraham would send Lazarus back to them as a messenger but Abraham's reply was that **the**

Scriptures were all that they would ever have. He also reminded the rich man that if they would not believe **the Scriptures** that they would not believe one though he may come back from the dead. This is a solemn reminder that the Scripture, enlightened by the Holy Spirit, is all the revelation we will have to guide us to salvation and they are all sufficient for that very purpose.

In the account of the rich man and Lazarus (Luke 16: 19 – 31) Jesus reveals very emphatically that there are two parts to Hades, or the place of the departed dead. The rich man was in a place of torment and flames (verse 24). Abraham, along with Lazarus, is in Paradise and they are speaking across a **deep gulf** that no one can cross. It is revealed that the rich man was in a place of suffering and torment and Lazarus is now comforted (verse 25). Moreover, it is apparent that we all carry our **memory** over into eternity. Abraham called upon the rich man to "**remember.**" Therefore, Lazarus is in the presence of Abraham in **Paradise**, which is the full meaning of the term "Abraham's bosom." The rich man is in "Hades" which refers to the intermediate state of the wicked where they suffer torment before being finally cast into the lake of fire (Gehena) after the **Great White Throne** judgment where the justice of God will be authenticated.

We Must Understand

Jesus provides more understanding of the term when He was on the cross and said to one of the thieves who was repentant, "*...Assuredly, I say to you, today you will be with me in Paradise.*" (Luke 23: 43) The torment of Hell is very real but yet he can remember his **rejection** of the **Scriptures**. He will also remember all of the blessings lost. He is now pleading for such a simple thing as a drop of water. In Hell, there is no exit for him because of that great gulf that no one can cross. His assignment to Hell is eternal. One of the greatest agonies of Hell is that of **despair** when the inhabitants **remember** the opportunities for eternal life that were lost through indifference. There is no neutrality about Jesus. To know about Him necessitates a decision. In fact, Jesus stated plainly that there will be degrees of punishment in Hell. He asserts that the person who knows the Lord's will but does not do it will be punished more severely than the person who did not know but did commit sin. Jesus said, "*And that servant who knew his master's will, and did not prepare himself or do according to his will, shall be beaten with many stripes. However, he who did not know, yet committed things worthy of stripes, shall be beaten with few. For everyone to whom much is given from him much will be required; and to whom much has been committed, of him they will ask the more.*" (Luke 12: 47-48) Again, man will be punished according to the **light against which he sinned**.

Chapter Seven
Why the New Birth?

Why is it so necessary that we experience the New Birth? Again, the Apostle John is careful to convey to us the very clear and wonderful teachings of Jesus Himself as He reports the visit of Nicodemus who came to Jesus by night. He was in the midst of assurance conveyed to Jesus that he and others knew that Jesus was a teacher who had come from God because no one could do the signs and miracles that Jesus did unless God was with Him. Jesus' response to him was, *"Most assuredly I say to you, unless one is born again, he cannot see the Kingdom of God."* (John 3:3) Jesus made it clear that the only way to enter into the Kingdom of God is by the New Birth. The term used in the New Testament for the New Birth is **gennethu anothen** (γεννηθύ άνωθεν). The word **anothen** actually indicates "from above." It is not a fleshly birth but a spiritual birth. It is an act of God in conferring upon believers the nature and disposition of "children" of God. John made that clear in his first chapter when he said, *"As many as received Him, to them gave He the right to become children of God, to those who believe in His name: who were born, not of blood, nor of the will of the flesh, nor the will of man, but of **God**."* (John 1: 12-13) John has made it clear that it is not a result of the flesh or of man but of **God**. Jesus clarified it to Nicodemus when He said, *"That which is born of the flesh is flesh, and that which is born of the spirit is spirit."* (John 3: 6) If we are to be children of God and a part of the family of God, then we must experience this **spiritual birth from above**! As Jesus explained to the woman at the well, *"**God is a spirit**, and those who worship Him **must** worship Him in **spirit** and truth."* (John 4: 23) That is the only way we can have a **relationship with God.** It is what is involved in reconciliation. In his pleading with the Corinthians Paul said, "... *God was in Christ* **reconciling** *the world to Himself, not imputing their trespasses to them, and has committed to us the word of reconciliation. Therefore, we are ambassadors for Christ, as though God were pleading through us: we implore you on Christ's behalf, be reconciled to God, for He made Him who knew no* **sin** *to be sin for us, that we might become the righteousness of God in Him."* (II Corinthians 5: 19-21) It is through the New Birth that we become Children of God, a part of God's family and we who were sinful and enemies of God are reconciled to Him through the **death of Christ at Calvary.** As we believe in Him, we become a part of the family of God. **There is not a more precious truth in the entire universe than that!**

The Process

Nicodemus was confused by Jesus' statement. He asked the obvious question of the natural man when he asked, *"How can a man be born when he is old? Can he enter a second time into his mother's womb and be born?"* Nicodemus was basically asking how a person could experience two **natural** births. Jesus assured him that the second birth is not a natural birth when He said, *"...unless one is born of the* **water** *and the* **Spirit**, *he cannot enter into the Kingdom of God."* Of course, the water birth is a natural birth. Every mother who has given birth to a child knows the process. There is first the breaking of the water followed by the birth of the child. It is referred to as a "water birth" as opposed to a "dry birth." In those days, it was very, very difficult to save a child of "dry birth" although, in modern medicine, children of dry birth are routinely saved. Jesus, however, said that the natural birth does not redeem the soul because that which is **born of the flesh** is **still flesh** and that is all it will ever be unless there is a spiritual birth. Nicodemus was apparently showing signs of incredulity, which Jesus dealt with by saying, *"Do not marvel that*

*I said to you, 'Ye must be born again.' The wind blows where it wishes, and you hear the sound of it, but cannot tell where it comes from and where it goes. So is everyone who is born of the **Spirit**."* The word that is translated "Spirit" is **pneumatos** (πνευματος). The root word is **pneuma** (ννευμα). The word denotes wind and is akin to the word **pneo** (πνεο) which means to breathe or to blow. Jesus is telling Nicodemus that there is a certain mystery about the new birth that cannot be explained or understood in human terms. It can only be understood **spiritually**. The birth of the Spirit, like the wind, is invisible to the human eye – non-material but powerful. For instance, the wind can drive a great ship at sea or it can cool a person in the evening after a hot sultry day. Sometimes, the wind can be so strong that it turns into a hurricane or a tornado. Again, the wind has been "harnessed" by many people for decades in order to pump water with the use of windmills. In the olden days, people in areas with a favorable wind velocity used wind to generate electricity, which charged batteries that would give them DC current in their houses. Some wind turbines are still used in various ways. With all that we understand about wind, there is still a mystery about it. We say this to emphasize the fact that a person does not have to understand everything about God in order to put his **faith** in God. We can be redeemed from sin and placed on the way to Heaven even though we may not understand everything about God. A form of the word is **theopneustos** (θεοπνευστος) and is used to describe the inspiration of Scripture or to convey the truth that the Scripture is "***God breathed***" (II Timothy 3: 16).

A Living Soul

When God created man, He *"Breathed into his nostrils the breath of life; and man became a **living being**"* or, as the King James Version puts it, he became a *"**living soul**."* That is not said of any other life form. It was not said of any animal, bird, or fish. Man was **unique**. Man is a **living soul**. That is the **spiritual** part of man that no other living creature has (Genesis 2: 7). It is in this way that man was created in the **image of God** (Genesis 1: 26-27). It is because of this truth that we can have a relationship with God because, as pointed out earlier, "*God is Spirit.*" (John 4: 24) That is the reason that Jesus told Nicodemus that one could not even see the Kingdom of God without that Spiritual birth. It is only at the Spiritual level that we can commune with God.

The Question

The question of Nicodemus was, "*How can these things be?*" (John 3: 9) In response Jesus gently chided Nicodemus when He asked, "*Are you the teacher of Israel, and do not know these things?*" Jesus is communicating to Nicodemus that he should have understood the need of a Spiritual birth as a teacher of Israel. It is possible to simply teach religion by rote with no Spiritual content and that was the kind of world Jesus came into. Very few of the religious leaders had any concept of the need for a Spiritual birth and a **Spiritual relationship** with God. Many have interpreted Jesus' next pronouncement as evidence that Nicodemus was never saved. It is hard for us to know these things because we know that he was active in burying Jesus but, of course, burying Him does not indicate a loyalty to Jesus or a submission to His Lordship. Jesus simply said to him, "*Most assuredly, I say to you, we speak what we know and testify what we have seen, and you* ***do not receive our witness.***" Jesus further posed the question to Nicodemus that if he could not believe earthly things, how would he believe Heavenly things.

Nicodemus lived in a world that was a pagan world filled with claims of pagan gods and goddesses. They believed that these pagan deities had become divine, and had ascended to heaven.

210

Jesus completely squelched that misguided notion. There were temples to pagan gods all over the middle-eastern world. Jesus presses His point that **none** of the claims of those gods and goddesses was valid. He informed him that, *"No one has ascended to Heaven but He who came down from Heaven, that is, the Son of Man who is in Heaven."* (Verse 13) Jesus then presents to Nicodemus the formula for that new birth when He said, *"For God so loved the world that He gave His only begotten Son, that whoever believes in Him should not perish but have everlasting life."* (John 3: 16) He further impressed upon Nicodemus that the sin, which would send a soul into a lost eternity, is that of **unbelief**. Jesus declared forever that, *"He who believes in Him is not condemned; but he who does not believe is condemned **already**,"* because *"**he has not believed** in the name of the only begotten Son of God."* (John 3:18)

Thus, Jesus lays out plainly to Nicodemus the reason that anyone is ever lost. The only reason anyone is ever lost is simply because they **will not believe in Jesus Christ**. Those who do not believe are condemned **already**! It is not that someone has to commit some heinous or nefarious act in order to be lost. Again, the thing that causes anyone to be lost is **unbelief**!

Elements of Salvation

God's part in our salvation is **grace**. Grace is the unmerited favor of God. Jesus had chided Nicodemus for his lack of understanding concerning the salvation process even though he was a teacher of Israel because the process of redemption had started back in the Book of Genesis at the time of creation. In Genesis 3: 15 we have the process known as the protoevangelium (sometimes erroneously spelled protevangelium). This is the first **good news (gospel)** about Christ. The serpent who introduced Eve to evil and tempted her was condemned by God to crawl upon his belly. The **Messiah** is identified as the "seed" of the woman. That could only be applied to Mary who gave birth to Jesus as a virgin because we know that the woman never carries the **seed** (sperm) but the **egg**. This is the only reference in Scripture concerning the **seed of woman**. Jesus, the Messiah, was born of Mary alone. Because of Satan's activity, there would be enmity between the seed of the woman and Satan. The seed of the woman would bruise or crush Satan's head and he would bruise the heel of her seed. We see then, that from the very Garden of Eden the salvation of man was provided. The **grace** of God was already operative.

God created man to be free. He was not to be an automaton. He would make choices. However, early man chose evil and debauchery. Man became so evil that God determined to destroy the earth by flood but there was one man and his family who walked uprightly before God and the Bible tells us in Genesis 6:8 that " *...Noah found* **grace** *in the eyes of the Lord.*" Because God extended His grace to Noah, he was spared the destruction of the earth through the flood. God gave him instructions in the building of the Ark by which he and his family were saved from the flood. Simon Peter recognized God's active grace in sparing Noah and his family from the flood because Noah was a *"preacher of righteousness"* but the flood came in on the world of the ungodly. (II Peter 2: 5)

God's Goodness

It was a promise of God voiced by the Psalmist who said, *"The Lord will give grace and glory. No good thing will be withheld from those who walk uprightly."* (Psalm 84: 11) When Zerubbabel was rebuilding the temple, God's promise to him was that He would remove the obstacles from his building of the temple and that he would complete the task with shoutings of *"grace, grace unto it."* (Zechariah 4: 7)

God's grace came to its' fruition in the birth of Jesus Christ our Lord. Keeping in mind that grace is the unmerited **favor** of God, we look forward to the annunciation by the angel Gabriel to Mary concerning our Lord's birth. The angel said to Mary, *"Rejoice highly favored one, the Lord is with you; blessed are you among women."* (Luke 1: 28) However, the angel was not finished! In verse 30 we read, *"Then the angel said to her 'Do not be afraid, Mary, for you have found favor with God."* It was then that he announced to her that she would conceive in her womb, bring forth a son, and call His name Jesus. Moreover, the angel assured her that the Holy Spirit would come upon her and the power of the highest would overshadow her **so that the holy one** who was to be born of her would be called the *"**Son of God**."* (Verse 34)

The Grace of Jesus

Then, the grace of God further came to fruition in the writings of the beloved disciple, John, who tells us that the "Word became flesh and dwelt among us, and we beheld His glory, the glory as of the only begotten of the Father, full of **grace** and **truth**." (John 1: 14) John came to the pinnacle of it all when he said, "...of His **fullness** have we all **received**, and **grace** for **grace**." (Verse 16) He further reminds us that the law came through Moses but "**Grace** and **truth** came through Jesus Christ." This reminds us that Jesus in the very beginning of the world was a part of the **triune God** and participated with God in the creation of all things (John 1: 1-4). It was the Apostle Paul who declared it emphatically and supported what John had written about the new birth (John 1: 12-13) when he said, "For by **grace** have you been **saved** through **faith**, and that (salvation) not of yourselves; it is the gift of God, not of works, lest anyone should boast." (Ephesians 2: 8-9)

That Word Grace

The word grace is translated from the Greek root word **charis** (χαρις). It literally means, "that which bestows or occasions pleasure, delight or causes favorable regard." A kindly act or graciousness, loving kindness, and good will generally proceed from the loving or friendly disposition. It is bestowed without regard to the recipient's worthiness or personal achievements. Thus, in regard to God's redemptive act, it is bestowed without regard of the ability of the recipient to reciprocate. Thus, on the part of the receiver it is bestowed with a sense of mercy. It is an inexorable truth that grace is that channel through which God deals with man in the midst of a corrupt and evil world, just as it was through grace that He dealt with Noah (Genesis 6: 8). Even when Israel was disobedient God still extended His grace and promised a new covenant. Grace came to its' pinnacle when Jesus Christ conquered sin, death and Hell on the cross of Calvary. When man understands God's grace, He gives new meaning to that powerful phrase in John 3 in which Jesus said to Nicodemus, "*As Moses lifted up the serpent in the wilderness, even so must the Son of Man be lifted up, that whosoever believes in Him should not perish but have eternal life.*" (John 3: 14-15) Jesus also declared, "*... this is the* **condemnation**, *that the light has come into the world, and men loved darkness rather than light, because their deeds were evil. For everyone practicing evil hates the light and does not come to the light, lest his deeds should be exposed.*" (John 3: 19-20)

Man's Part

While grace may be understood as God reaching down to man and offering salvation without any merit on the part of man, faith is man reaching up to God. It is that by which we **appropriate salvation**. The Greek word for faith is pistis (πιστις). Its' primary meaning is "a firm persuasion or a conviction based upon hearing." In the New Testament, it always refers to faith in God or Jesus Christ. In the New Testament usage, it also has the connotation of the **thing that is believed.** It is a belief not necessarily dependent upon proof. The disciples once came to Jesus asking, *"Lord, increase our faith."* (Luke 17: 5) It was on that occasion that the Lord told them that if they had the faith of a grain of mustard seed, they could say to the mulberry tree, *"'Be pulled up by the roots and be planted in the sea,' and it would obey you."* The most important thing that faith ever does, however, is to bring salvation to the life of sinful man. Thus, faith and belief can never be separated.

In the eleventh chapter of Hebrews, we have that great chapter on faith. The chapter begins with a definition of faith. It states emphatically that faith is the *"substance of things hoped for, the evidence of things not seen."* To be sure, faith is not a blind leap in the dark. It is **substance and evidence**. The word that is translated substance is hupostasis (ὑποσασις). It refers to foundational things or the basis of our hope in Christ. It is that solid, unshakable confidence in God. It is our trust that He is **faithful**. It might be understood as the solid rock upon which we stand that Jesus spoke of in Matthew 16:18. As pointed out earlier, Jesus is stating that the rock upon which He will build His Church is **Himself** and it refers to **bedrock**. The term "**evidence**" is translated from the word elienchos (ελιενχος). It carries with it the connotation of proof. Evidence always provides proof. You look at rustling leaves of a tree and you know that the wind is blowing because you see the evidence of it in the rustling of the leaves. When you see the rain puddles after a rain, you know that those puddles provide evidence that rain has fallen. Therefore, we stand on a firm foundation in Jesus Christ and we see the evidence of His work in the world as we observe lives changed, prayers answered and churches edified because of our faith in proclaiming the **good news of Jesus Christ**.

About Evidence

It is through our **faith** that is founded on the unshakable **evidence** that God has provided all around us that we understand the framing of the world by the very **Word of God** so that *"things which are seen were not made of things which do appear."* (Hebrews 11: 3) This is followed by a chronicling of Old Testament saints who were enabled by the power of God to accomplish great things for God because of their **great faith**. In fact, the writer of Hebrews pauses at 11: 6 to say, *"Without faith it is **impossible** to please Him: for he that cometh to God **must believe** that He is and that He is a rewarder of them that diligently seek Him."*

In this beautiful chapter of Hebrews 11, we find the answer to questions that many young Americans raise. We often hear the question as to "What happened to the people of the Old Testament who believed in God but were born and died before Jesus came?" They were saved by **faith** just as we are saved by faith, the blood of Jesus Christ covered all of those saints who had gone before, and it covers all the saints who follow. We will never have to worry about what happened to the Old Testament saints because they were people of faith who believed God and obeyed Him. That is what God is looking for – people who will obey and serve Him by **faith**.

216

Repentance

Repentance is an integral and indispensable part of the salvation process. When John the Baptist, the forerunner of Jesus, began preaching in the Wilderness of Judea his message was, *"Repent, for the Kingdom of Heaven is at hand!"* (Matthew 3: 2) Again, at the conclusion of Peter's sermon on the Day of Pentecost the people were *"cut to the heart"* and they asked Peter and the other apostles, *"Men and Brethren, what shall we do?"* (Acts 2:37) Peter's answer to them was, *"Repent and let everyone of you be baptized in the name of Jesus Christ for the remission of sin; and ye shall receive the gift of the Holy Spirit."* (Acts 2: 38) When Paul was in Athens, he preached on Mars Hill. It was one of the great sermons of the New Testament. They had erected an idol to the **unknown god**. Paul's message was, *"The one whom you worship without knowing, Him I proclaim to you ...."* As he concluded his message Paul said, *"Truly, these times of ignorance God overlooked, but now commands all men everywhere to **repent**."* (Acts 17: 23 – 30) In the Revelation, the Apostle John records the message of Jesus to the seven churches of Asia. The church of Laodicea was a backslidden church but they thought they were rich and wealthy and had need of nothing but were not aware that they were wretched, miserable, poor, blind, and naked. The Lord's charge to them was, *"As many as I **love**, I **rebuke** and **chasten**. Therefore, be zealous and **repent**."* (Revelation 3: 19) The word repent is translated from the Greek word metanoeo (μετανοεω). It means to change one's mind and purpose. It also means to turn about and walk in the opposite direction. In the New Testament, it always involves a change for the better. It appears in Luke 9 times, in Acts 5 times and in the Revelation 12 times. In the New Testament, the act of repentance involves a turning **from sin** and a turning **to God**.

Jesus' Ministry

After the Wilderness temptation, Jesus, like John the Baptist, began His earthly ministry and it is summed up well in Matthew 4: 17, which says, *"From that time Jesus began to preach and to say, 'Repent, for the Kingdom of Heaven is at hand.'"* That was a **basic theme** of His ministry.

We see then that if Jesus began His earthly ministry preaching repentance and preached it repeatedly, even calling upon the churches of the Revelation to repent (except for Smyrna and Philadelphia). The cleansing process is so intertwined with the New Birth that the two can never be separated because **repentance** is a **part** of the **New Birth**. Repentance and forgiveness is a wonderfully cleansing process that leaves the believer clean and unshackled by sin before the Lord. Repentance and forgiveness is something that the believer seeks repeatedly in his life. John made that clear in his first letter when he said, *"If we confess our sins, He is faithful and just to forgive us our sins and to cleanse us from all unrighteousness."* John had made it clear that we will not reach a state of sinless perfection when he wrote, *"If we say that we have no sin, we deceive ourselves and the truth is not in us."* In his last years his word to believers was, *"My little children, these things I write to you that you might not sin. And if anyone sins we have an **advocate** with the **Father, Jesus Christ the righteous**. And He, Himself, is the **propitiation** for our sins, and not for ours only but also for the whole world."* (I John 2:1-2) John makes it clear and includes himself by using the inclusive pronoun when he says, *"If **we say** that we **have** no sin."* He pleads with men not to sin but he understands the frailty of man and declares, *"If anyone sins, we have an **advocate** with the Father, **Jesus Christ** the righteous."* Christ was our **propitiation** meaning that He paid the price and penalty for sin at Calvary and for all mankind. Those who believe in Him come under His **protective shed blood**. Thus, man is reconciled to God because Jesus gave **His sinless life sacrificially** for our sin, thus annulling the power of sin to separate us from our God. The Greek word here is hilasmos (ἱλασμός). It indicates a means whereby sin is **covered and remitted**. Through His expiatory sacrifice at Calvary, He became the personal means by whom God shows mercy to the sinner who believes on Christ as the **eternal sacrifice** for sin. John makes it clear that His sacrifice was for *"the whole world."* This means that everyone in the world is offered freely the forgiveness of sin but they must exercise their faith in laying hold of it. **No one is, by Divine predetermination**, excluded from the scope of God's mercy but the efficacy of propitiation is only for those who **repent and believe**. It is in that way that Calvary became an eternal expression of God's love toward man and thus, calls upon Christians, to love one another. John amplifies that great truth in I John 4: 10 when he said, *"In this is love, not that we loved God, but that He loved us and sent His Son to be the propitiation for our sins."* He further points out that " ... *if God so loved us, we also ought to love one another."* It never gets any clearer than that. How can we know that He abides in us and we abide in Him? It is *"because **He** has given us of His **Spirit**."* (Verse 13)

Results of the New Birth

The result of the New Birth is a stark, earth shaking and dramatic change in the life of the individual. Again, we go to John who reports what Jesus said about it when He said, *"Most assuredly, I say to you, he who **hears** my word and **believes** in Him who sent me **has** everlasting life, and **shall not** come into judgment, but **is passed** from **death** into **life**."* (John 5: 24) Therefore, Jesus astounded the world by pointing out that the New Birth changes one from a state of **death** to a state of **life** and spares him from eternal judgment or, as the King James translation puts it, *"condemnation."* Man, living in this state of death, cannot receive the things of God. There is no spiritual insight or perception in him. That is the truth that the Apostle Paul pointed out in I Corinthians 2: 14 when he said, *"... the natural man does **not** receive the things of the Spirit of God, for they are **foolishness** to him; nor can he know them, because they are spiritually discerned."* Man, living in that natural state of death, cannot in any way affect his own salvation. As hard as he may try, it is all in vain. That is what Paul pointed out in his letter to Titus when he said, *"Not by works of righteousness which we have done, but according to His mercy he saved us, through the washing of regeneration and renewing of the Holy Spirit."* (Titus 3: 5) Man, while living in that state of death, may do many things that are perceived by the world to be good or righteous but in God's sight, those works are nothing more than *"filthy rags."* (Isaiah 64: 6)

Abusive Man

Most often, man in the state of death is abusive of the things of God. He may take the name of God in vain. His speech may be filthy. He often abuses himself with drink or narcotics. He often abuses his family by beating his children or even his spouse. The same thing may be true of the woman who is living in that state of death. Moreover, man living in that state of death is often **abusive** to society. He breaks the law. Prisons are full of people who are living in that state of death. It is a miserable existence. It is a purposeless life. The body is functioning but the soul is **dead**. Paul refers to it as being a life of death when he said, *"And you He made **alive** who were **dead in trespasses and sins,** in which you once **walked** according to the **course of this world**, according to the prince of the power of the air, the spirit who now works in the **sons of disobedience**, among whom also we all once conducted ourselves in the lusts of the flesh, fulfilling the desires of the flesh* *and of the mind, and were **by nature** children of wrath, just as the others."* (Ephesians 2: 1-3) He further pointed out that God, who is rich in mercy and because of His great love for us, even when we were dead in trespasses and sins *"made us alive together with Christ (by grace you have been saved) ..."* (Ephesians 2: 4-5)

New Creations

Paul described this dramatic change that is wrought by the new birth to the Corinthians when he said, *"Therefore, if anyone is in Christ, he is a **new creation**; old things have passed away; behold, all things have become new."* (II Corinthians 5: 17) He refers to the spiritual transformation that takes place when a person is born again. The Christian is now a new person as opposed to the old person that he was before he experienced the New Birth. Paul describes the change in graphic terms to the Galatians when he said, *"Now the works of the flesh are evident, which are: adultery, fornication, uncleanliness, licentiousness, idolatry, sorcery, hatred, contentions, jealousies, outbursts of wrath, selfish ambitions, dissensions, heresies, envy, murders, drunkenness, revelries, and the like; of which I tell you beforehand just as I told you in time past, that those who practice such things will not inherit the Kingdom of God."* Then, he lists the **fruits of the Spirit** that reflect that metamorphosis of character that takes place when we are born again when he says, *"But the fruit of the Spirit is love, joy, peace, long suffering, kindness, goodness, faithfulness, gentleness, self-control. Against such, there is no law and those who are Christ's have crucified the flesh with its passions and desires. If we live in the Spirit, let us also walk in the Spirit."* (Galatians 5: 19-25) This gives us a word picture of the **difference that Christ makes** in a person's life!

Life in Him

When we understand these things, we understand more clearly, what John was talking about when he said in the beginning of his prologue, *"In Him was **life**, and the life was the **light** of men."* (John 1: 4) It could not be stated any more profoundly than Jesus stated it in John 6: 63 when He said, *"It is the **Spirit** who gives **life**; the flesh profits nothing. The **words** that I speak to you are **Spirit** and they are **life**."* Jesus reiterated this truth in John 8: 12 when He said, *"I am the light of the world, he who follows me shall not walk in darkness, but have the **light of life**."* John never tired of the theme of life. In I John 5: 12 he makes it clear and plain when he said, *"He who has the **son has life**; he who does not have the Son of God **does not have life**."* In the closing chapter of the Revelation John says, *"And whoever desires, let him take the **water** of **life** freely."* (Revelation 22: 17) The most blessed truth that we can ever know is to know that our names our written in the *"Lamb's Book of **Life**."* (Revelation 21: 27)

Thus, we see the **blessedness** and the **necessity** of the **New Birth**. It changes us from a dead individual who is not worthy of the Lord's presence, or Heaven, or the joys thereof to a person who not only bears fruit in this life and becomes a joy and help to others but a person who is worthy of a **place in Heaven** and fellowship with our Lord for eternity. That is the reason that Christians sing so many hymns of thanksgiving and praise for the change that came when Jesus came into our hearts. The New Birth? Yes, it is a necessity and it is also the most wonderful experience of any life. Back in the 1800's William T. Sleeper wrote about it when he said:

"A ruler once came to Jesus by night
To ask Him the way of salvation and light
The Master made answer in words true and plain
Ye must be born again."
"Ye children of men **attend** to the **word**

So solemnly uttered by Jesus the Lord
And let not this message to you be in vain
Ye must be born again."
"Oh ye who would enter that glorious rest
And sing with the ransomed the song of the blest
A life everlasting if ye would obtain
Ye must be born again."
"A dear one in Heaven thy heart yearns to see
At the beautiful gate may be watching for thee
Then list to the note of this solemn refrain
Ye must be born again."

There is nothing this writer could say that would improve upon that invitation. Our life on this earth is but a short period of probation in which we have opportunity to prepare for eternity with our Lord in Heaven and there is no other way to make that preparation than through the New Birth. What **Jesus** said to Nicodemus that night is **still true and will forever be true**!

Chapter Eight
Is There Really A Holy Spirit?

Yes, a thousand times yes, there really is a Holy Spirit but we need to understand that the Holy Spirit is more than a dove in a stained glass window. That is a beautiful symbol of the Holy Spirit but it is not the essence of the Holy Spirit. It is important that young adults understand that the Holy Spirit is a **person**. The Holy Spirit is not simply a presence or a power. The Holy Spirit is not a fairy like woman dressed in sheer gauzy apparel who is a bit flighty as has been portrayed in some modern literature. The Holy Spirit is a part of the Trinity. We are Trinitarians and we must never allow ourselves to be dissuaded from this great Biblical truth. We believe in God the **Father**, God the **Son** and God the **Holy Spirit**. We must understand this critically important Biblical truth. Some Christians have shied away from this great Biblical doctrine because a few have abused it but we should never abandon Biblical truth because a few charlatans have abused it. Yes, the Holy Spirit does have great power and an overmastering presence in the life of Christians. Yes, He does exercise influence in our lives but it is critically important that we understand the person and nature of the Holy Spirit.

The Trinity and Its' Purpose

The Trinity is well established in the very first line of the first book of the Bible. In Genesis 1: 1 the Scripture reads, *"In the beginning God created the Heavens and the Earth."* The Hebrew word for God (Elohim) is a **plural** noun. This **plural** noun is followed by a **singular** verb (bara). This structure makes it clear that we worship, serve, and are guided by a triune God. We are monotheistic Trinitarians. Moreover, the Holy Spirit was active in creation. It was the **Spirit** of God that moved upon the face of the waters (Genesis 1: 2). The Holy Spirit was active right along with Jesus Christ in creation. John made it plain when he wrote, *"All things were made through Him and without Him was not anything made that was made."* (John 1: 1) In the account concerning the creation of man in Genesis 1: 26 the Scriptures declare, *"Then God said, 'Let **us** make man in **our** image, according to **our** likeness ....'"* The plural pronoun *"**us**"* is in perfect harmony with the plural noun for God (Elohim) which again underscores the **Trinity.** So, it becomes abundantly clear that God the **Father**, God the **Son** and God the **Holy Spirit** were all active in creation. As John points out, *"These three are one."* (I John 5:7)

Characteristics

As we think of the characteristics of the Holy Spirit, it is critically important that we comprehend His nature. In the Roman letter, Paul tells us that the Holy Spirit has a mind and therefore can **think** (Romans 8: 27). There can never be any doubt when Paul says, *"Now he who searches the hearts **knows** what the **mind** of the **Spirit** is."* Having a mind means that the Spirit has knowledge. In I Corinthians 2: 11 we have another declaration that says, *"For what man knows the things of a man except the **spirit** of the man which is in him? Even so no one **knows** the **things of God** except the **Spirit** of God."* We see the activity of the Holy Spirit throughout the Old Testament. The word in the Old Testament that is translated "Spirit" (ruach) means breath, wind or spirit. That is important to understand as we look at Genesis 2: 7 concerning the creation of man, which tells us *"God **breathed** into his nostrils the **breath of life**; and man became a **living soul.**"* (KJV) This is not said of any animal creature but only of man and this is the thing that sets man apart from the Animal Kingdom. He is not just another form of animal life. He is a **living soul**. Thus, we see that the Holy Spirit is that part of the Trinity that represents the **outgoing energy of God** in the universe and in the **life of man**. The presence of the Holy Spirit is also synonymous with the presence of God (Psalm 139: 7).

In Exodus 31: 3 – 5 we learn that Bazaleel received gifts of the **Spirit** so that he understood and had knowledge of various kinds of workmanship or craftsmanship. When we move forward to Judges 14: 6 we learn that when a young lion roared against Samson *"... the **Spirit** of the Lord came mightily upon him, and he tore the lion apart as one would have torn apart a young goat though he had nothing in his hand ..."* Again, we find that the **Spirit** empowered Samson but when that Spirit left him, he was helpless. What a lesson for us today! (Judges 16: 20)

When the Word of the Lord came to Zerubbabel it was that *"... not by might nor by power, but by **my Spirit**, says the Lord of hosts."* (Zachariah 4: 6) It was Isaiah who prophesied of Jesus that, *"The **Spirit** of the Lord shall rest upon him, the **Spirit** of wisdom and understanding. The **Spirit** of counsel and might. The **Spirit** of knowledge and of the fear of the Lord."* (Isaiah 11: 2) That prophecy was fulfilled at the baptism of Jesus. (Matthew 3: 16) Again, we see the **nature** of the Holy Spirit is that of **empowering people** for **service** and ministry. What a blessing!

Function of the Spirit

In the Old Testament, the thing that qualified a prophet to prophesy was that the **Spirit** of the **Lord** would rest upon him (Numbers 11: 25 – 26). These are recurring themes throughout the Old Testament. It was the empowering of the Spirit of God that made the difference in the life of the man of God. Without that power, he is as helpless as Samson was after his disobedience to

227

the Lord. After his prayer of confession, David recognized the necessity of the **Holy Spirit** to empower his life. He not only pleaded that the Lord would cleanse him of his sin but he pleaded, *"Do not **cast me away** from your presence and take not your **Holy Spirit** from me."* (Psalm 51: 11) He recognized that only the Holy Spirit could restore him to the joy of the Lord's salvation. It was the prophet Joel who gave the Word of the Lord concerning a day in the future when the Lord said, *"... I will pour out **my Sp**irit on all flesh; ..."* (Joel 2: 28) This was fulfilled on the Day of Pentecost. More about that later.

Only a few passages have been mentioned here and these passages by no means exhaust the work of the Holy Spirit in the Old Testament but they are designed to demonstrate that the Holy Spirit, as a part of the Trinity, has been at work from the beginning of creation even until now.

Can Be Grieved

Another characteristic of the Holy Spirit is that He is sensitive to the needs and behavior of man. For instance, Paul admonishes believers, *"Do not **grieve** the **Holy Spirit of God** by whom you were **sealed** for the **day of redemption.**"* (Ephesians 4: 30) This is done by ungodly behavior such as *"bitterness, and wrath, and anger, and clamor, and evil speaking, and ... malice."* (Ephesians 4: 31) As a part of the triune God, it is the Holy Spirit who is guarantor of our salvation. When we were saved after hearing the word of truth, we were *"... **sealed** with the **Holy Spirit** of promise."* (Ephesians 1: 13) It is also the Holy Spirit who will be the, *"**guarantee** of our inheritance until the **redemption** of the purchased possession, to the praise of His glory."* (Ephesians 1: 14)

Can Be Quenched

Moreover, the Holy Spirit can be **quenched**. The person of the Holy Spirit **will not force Himself upon us**. While He is sensitive to our needs and our behavior, it is possible for us to "*quench*" the Spirit. In the closing of the letter to the church at Thessalonica, Paul admonishes the believers that they "... **not quench the Spirit.**" (I Thessalonians 5: 19) This is an awesome thing that man is capable of doing. Therefore, we see that it is God, the Holy Spirit, who convicts us and brings us to salvation (John 3: 5; 16: 13). God the Holy Spirit seals our salvation. That means the transaction of our salvation is done and will never be undone. He provides the "*guarantee*" or **down payment** that assures the **completion** of our **salvation** in the Day of the Lord when He will return and receive us unto Himself.

The most important manifestation of the Holy Spirit in the history of redemption was His outpouring on the Day of Pentecost. It was on that day that the King of Kings through the Spirit **empowered His church** to do kingdom work. Thus began the formation of the earthly body of Christ. It is clear, however, that the condition and attitude of the church in the present day has changed remarkably. It seems that, in many cases, the presence of the Holy Spirit is absent from the work of the Church. That is sad because of the ministry of the Holy Spirit is purposely rejected.

He Is Our Mentor

When Jesus ascended from earth, He promised that He would send a comforter. That comforter is the **Holy Spirit.** He is our trusted counselor, guide, tutor, and coach. That is the basic meaning of the term "mentor." He is a mentor that will never give up on us. He will be with us forever. He will **indwell** us. He will

teach us. He will uncover the **mysteries** of the Faith for us. He produces spiritual character in us (Galatians 5: 22-23). He is our **encourager**. In that capacity, He uncovers and **reveals** to us the **truth of God**. We are reminded again, of what Jesus said when He said that, the Holy Spirit would *"guide you into all truth."* (John 16: 13) He teaches us how to discern what is right and what is wrong. We cannot receive that discernment anywhere else but from the **Holy Spirit of God**.

What He Means To Us

Apart from the Holy Spirit, we are like a ship without a rudder that is adrift in a raging storm. The **Holy Spirit** provides **everything we need** as followers of Christ. He is our **teacher** and **guide** concerning truth (John 16: 13). He is our **intercessor** before the throne of God (Romans 8: 26-27). The Holy Spirit gives us abundant **joy and peace** that passes understanding. (Philippians 4:7) He gives us **discernment** in ministry for the Lord Jesus Christ (Ephesians 4: 11-12; 6: 17). He provides **boldness** for our witness to the lost (I Timothy 3: 13). He gives us **power** (Zachariah 4: 6). He helps us to **live Godly** lives (Ezekiel 36: 27). He helps us to **pray** (Ephesians 6: 18).

The Scriptures that we have referred to here are simply to establish the fact that the Holy Spirit is a **person** who is a part of the **God/head**. It is not an exhaustive list by any means. It only serves to **illustrate**. We also seek to demonstrate that it is by the Holy Spirit that the energy of the **triune God** is dispatched to believers in the world today. The believer who understands these things has taken a **bold step** toward the status of a Spirit filled Christian.

Receiving the Spirit

While the Scripture doesn't give detailed instructions as to how we are to receive the Holy Spirit, the most instructive examples in Scripture involve **unity, waiting, prayer** and **supplication** (Acts 1: 14). In Luke's moving description of Jesus' ascension scene and after Jesus had given them a command to be His witnesses, Jesus assured them that He would *"send the promise of My Father upon you; but tarry in the city of Jerusalem* **until** *you are endued with* **power** *from* **on high.**" (Luke 24: 49) This promise, that Peter reminded the people about on the Day of Pentecost (Acts 2: 17), is a reference to Joel 2: 28 in which God says, "*I will pour out my Spirit on all flesh."* It means that there will be **no discrimination**. The Spirit will be available to all kindred and nations. It will be available to the young and the old, to men and women, to people of all classes and stations in life. No one will be **restricted** and no one will be **excluded**. Anyone who **desires** the **Spirit** can **receive** Him. Thus, Jesus declares for time and eternity, the absolute **necessity** and **centrality** of the **Holy Spirit** in carrying out His mission on earth. The mission of the Holy Spirit precedes the mission of the church. It is important that believers understand this. If the Holy Spirit is absent from the life of a Christian, any type of Christian discipleship is inconceivable. The Holy Spirit is the life giver. He is the personification of truth. He is the great unifier. He is the one who brings forth fruit in the Christian life. Without His **power,** there can be no effective witness in the life of the believer. When Jesus commanded the Apostles to tarry in the city of Jerusalem until they were endued with power from on high, the Luke passage was inexorably coupled with the first two chapters of the book of Acts. Our Heavenly Father's desire for us is to be **filled** with the **Holy Spirit's power** and be used for kingdom service. The Holy Spirit is not a "flash in the pan" kind of living. That truth is not negotiable. The believer who would live a victorious life must understand that he must rely solely on the presence and power of the Holy Spirit for successful kingdom living. Any other approach will fail.

Luke opens the book of Acts by addressing Theophilus, whom many believe to have been an official of Government, informing him that his former *"treatise,"* which was a reference to the Gospel of Luke, revealed *"all things Jesus **began** both to do and to teach."* The book of Acts reveals what Jesus **continued** to do through **Spirit** filled people. In Acts 1: 3, we have the only reference in the New Testament as to how long Jesus ministered on earth after His resurrection. It was for 40 days. During that period, Jesus established three critical truths that related to victorious Christian living.

First, He *"also presented Himself **alive** after suffering by many infallible proofs."* (Acts 1: 3) There must be absolutely no doubt that Jesus arose from the grave and conquered sin, death, and hell. If we count the Damascus Road appearance, there were at least 10 appearances of Christ after His resurrection that are recorded in the Scripture. The Apostle Paul enumerates some of His appearances and stated that He was seen *"by over 500 brethren at one time."* (I Corinthians 15: 6) His final appearance was to the Apostle Paul on the Damascus Road (Acts 9: 4 - 17) When Jesus made that final appearance to an earthly being, the light of the Lord blinded Saul so that he could not see for three days. Saul later received an infilling of the Holy Spirit through the ministry of Ananias at the home of Judas on the street called Straight in the city of Damascus. The **infallible** proofs refer to **indisputable** proofs. It is beyond any reasonable doubt that Jesus arose from the grave. Although Josephus, the highly revered Jewish historian, reported the resurrection of Jesus, we never need to appeal to any outside sources. All the evidence we need is in the Scripture and there is no empirical or historical evidence to the contrary. **Jesus**

is alive! The disciples had to be firmly convinced of His resurrection in order to be effective in their mission. Therefore, likewise, must believers today have a certainty in their heart if they are to live an effective Christian life. It is the **Holy Spirit** that makes Jesus real to us. Some of our greatest experiences as Christians come at Easter during the Sunrise services. As the sun comes up and takes away the darkness; the proclamation of "He is risen!" releases the power of the Holy Spirit; illuminating the purposes and plans of God for His people.

Second, Jesus taught them of the things pertaining to the Kingdom of God. In the Luke passage, Jesus *"opened their* **understanding***, that they might* **comprehend the Scriptures***."* Then He said to them, *"'Thus it is written, and thus it was necessary for Christ to suffer and to rise from the dead the third day, and that repentance and remission of sins should be preached in His name to all nations, beginning at Jerusalem'."* (Luke 24: 45 – 47) In Matthew 28 we have an additional word concerning His post-resurrection teachings when He said, *"All authority has been given to Me in heaven and on earth. Go therefore and make disciples of all nations, baptizing them in the name of the* **Father***, and of the* **Son***, and of the* **Holy Spirit,** *teaching them to* **observe all things** *that I have commanded you; and lo I am with you always, even to the end of the age."* (Matthew 28: 18-20) Here again, we have the teaching of Jesus concerning His **Sonship** and the **Trinity.** We are to be baptized in the name of the **Father**, the **Son**, and the **Holy Spirit**.

After we have lead believers to Christ, we have a teaching responsibility. We are to teach His followers **all** things that He has commanded us. There is never a place for a partial or halfhearted Gospel. We must never forget that the Gospel is good news. When believers are motivated by the Holy Spirit, they carry the greatest, most wonderful message ever given – Jesus saves! Jesus makes it clear that we are to declare the **whole counsel** of God and we are to never be ashamed of that message (Romans 1: 16). He has assured us, that in that process, He is always with us. How He is with us is through the person and power of the **Holy Spirit.**

Third, Jesus commanded the early believers in Jerusalem to wait upon the empowerment of the **Holy Spirit.** This is the only thing that works and without the power of the Holy Spirit, we can **do nothing.** He did not suggest that tolerance of sin in our midst would make us successful. He never even hinted that compromise would assist us in accomplishing His purposes

John's Record

It was on the evening of the resurrection day when the disciples were gathered together with the doors shut because they feared the Jews. On this occasion, we have two records of evidence that make the resurrection of Jesus an **infallible** truth. **First,** Jesus appeared in their midst even though the doors were shut. How could this be? We are talking about a part of the Godhead who created everything. There was a characteristic of His resurrection body that enabled Him to pass through closed doors. We do not understand all about that but that is as **infallible** as it gets! John was there and observed it all. What did he say about it? We find his answer in I John 3: 2 when he said, "*Beloved, now we are children of God; and it has not yet been revealed what we shall be, but we **know** that when He is revealed, **we shall be like Him**, for we shall see Him as He is.*" That means we will have a **complete** understanding of His body as well as **our eternal bodies.** Paul addressed the matter in I Corinthians 13: 12 when he said, "*For now we see in a mirror dimly, but then face to face. Now I know in part, but then I shall know just as I also am known.*" Jesus showed them His "*hands and His side.*" They were gladdened by this experience. **Second,** it is to that group of fearful disciples on the resurrection day that Jesus said, "*Peace to you! As the Father has sent me, I also send you.*" It was on that occasion that He gave them a foretaste of Pentecost, which was a few days ahead for them when He *"breathed on them, and said to them, 'Receive the Holy Spirit.'"* (John 20: 20 – 22) How much more powerful could it get? It should be noted that this was the first action of Jesus toward His disciples after His resurrection, which should tell us volumes about the **importance** of the **Holy Spirit** in the service of the Lord and the spread of His gospel after His **resurrection** and **ascension**.

Pentecost

After the ascension of Jesus the disciples of Jesus tarried for ten days *"with one accord in prayer and supplication."* (Acts 1: 14) At the end of 10 days was the Feast of Pentecost. The word "Pentecost" simply means "50th". It took place 50 days after the Passover. The Feast was a very popular feast because it was a celebration of the completion of grain harvest as well as a celebration of the receiving of the law of Moses on Sinai. It was sometimes known as the "Feast of Weeks" (Exodus 34: 22; Deuteronomy 16: 10). It was referred to in Exodus 23: 16 as the "Feast of Harvest". All males were expected to attend this Feast. This accounts for the fact that there were *"devout men out of every nation under heaven"* who were present (Acts 2: 5).

Many different languages were represented on the day of Pentecost. This is the circumstance that prompted the need for the miracle of translation when the disciples began to speak to the people. The people understood in **their own native tongue**. People in such situations tend to gather together in groups of their own language. It is apparent that the disciples went to speak to those various language groups and the language groups could hear the disciples in their own **tongue** or their own **language.** It was a miraculous divine plan on the day of Pentecost that would send the Gospel message to all parts of the world. This great ministry **happened because *"The Spirit gave them utterance."*** (Acts 2: 4) **This was another ministry of the Holy Spirit of God**. In the upper room the disciples had experienced the power of the Holy Spirit when Jesus breathed on them. Later, on the day of Pentecost there was the sound of a mighty rushing **wind** and the appearance of tongues of fire. Wind and fire appear in the Old Testament as signs of the presence of God. When God delivered the Philistines into the hands of David, he commanded David to go around them and wait at the Mulberry trees until he should hear *"the **sound** of marching in the tops of the Mulberry trees,"* and that is when he should attack (II Samuel 5: 24). In Psalm 104: 3 the mighty God is described as one who *"walks on the wings of the wind."* When God called Moses to deliver His people He appeared to Moses in a flame of fire in a bush that was not consumed. When Moses drew near the burning bush, God spoke to him and commanded him to remove his shoes for he was standing on holy ground in the **presence** of the Lord (Exodus 3: 2-5). When the Israelites were delivered from Egypt, God guided them with a cloud by day and pillar of **fire** by night (Exodus 13: 21-22).

Prophecy Fulfilled

When Peter stood to preach he stood in recognition that the disciples were *"all filled with the **Holy Spirit**"* and that this was a fulfillment of Joel's prophecy recorded in Joel 2: 28. Pentecost was such an usual event because it was bathed in the power of the Holy Spirit. As a result the people were *"cut to the heart,"* (Acts 2: 37) and asked Peter and the rest of the apostles: *"What shall we do?"* At the house of Cornelius the **Holy Spirit** fell upon the hearers of Peter's sermon before they were baptized (Acts 10: 44-47). This power came upon the disciples because they had waited and *"continued with one accord in **prayer and supplication**."* (Acts 1: 14)

We All Receive

We all receive the Holy Spirit when we are saved as is clearly taught in I Corinthians 12: 13. The indwelling of the Holy Spirit refers to our salvation. It was George Whitfield who said that the indwelling of the Spirit is "the common privilege of all believers." There is a difference, however, between "**indwelling**" and "**infilling**". It is the Holy Spirit who convicts us of our sin and our need for salvation. As a result of that conviction, we are brought to a point of regeneration. We are saved! Then the Holy Spirit takes up residence in our lives and, as a result, **seals us for eternity**. In the Book of Acts, Jesus instructed the disciples to remain in Jerusalem and wait for the Holy Spirit's power to come upon them (Acts 1:4). It is clear, that without the Holy Spirit, there is no salvation. It is not an option in the Christian life (Romans 8: 9). In the latter part of verse 9 Paul makes it clear that "*If anyone does not have the **Spirit** of Christ, he is not His.*"

Infillings

While Jesus breathed upon them and they received the Holy Spirit (John 20: 22), He told them 40 days later just before His ascension that they would be "***baptized** with the Holy Spirit not many days from now.*" (Acts 1: 5) In His final words to them while on earth, he said, "*Ye shall receive **power** when the Holy Spirit has come upon you and you shall be witnesses unto Me in **Jerusalem**, and in **Judea** and **Samaria**, and to the **end of the earth**.*" (Verse 8) This was another **infilling** of the Holy Spirit of which they would experience many. This is the baptism that was predicted by John the Baptist in John 1: 33. When Peter and John were hauled before Annas and his kindred, Peter "***filled** with the Holy Spirit*" assured them that the man was made whole by the resurrected Christ (Acts 4: 8). The term "**infilling**" refers to absolute control. When

237

we are filled with the Holy Spirit, we come under the absolute control of the Holy Spirit. This is what Paul was getting at when he wrote to Timothy saying, "**stir up** *the gift of God which* **is in you** *through the laying on of my hands.*" (I Timothy 1: 6) That **gift** was the **gift of the Spirit**. Timothy possessed that gift because of his indwelling **faith** (I Timothy 1: 5). While Paul waited in Athens for Timothy and Silas, the Bible says that "*His spirit was* **stirred in him** *when he saw the city wholly given to idolatry.*" (Acts 17: 16 KJV) These are infillings of the spirit. They may also happen to the believer in other ways such as in prayer or Bible study or the hearing of the spoken word or in times of worship.

The Spirit's Control

In Ephesians 5: 18 Paul is addressing Christians who have been saved and who already have the Holy Spirit, but he urged them saying, "*And do not be* **drunk with wine,** *in which is dissipation; but* **filled with the Spirit.**" In this passage, Paul is drawing an analogy between intoxication by alcohol and control of the Holy Spirit. To be drunk on wine means that the alcohol affects every part of the body. A person's walk, speech, thoughts, sight and hearing are all affected by alcohol in the body. Even so, when one is **filled with the Spirit**, it profoundly means that every action is brought under the Spirit's control. When the Spirit has absolute control in our lives, **He possesses us!** It is also true that if the **Spirit** possesses us, Satan **cannot!** Thus, it is the Holy Spirit who repeatedly infills us and directs us in our service to the Lord, Jesus Christ! The Scriptures also make it clear that the Holy Spirit is ours for the **asking** (Luke 11: 13). Not only must we ask but we must **ask believing** (Matthew 21: 22). This all happens just as it did on the day of Pentecost, by "***prayer and supplication.***"

Results

There were some earth shaking results of the baptism of the Holy Spirit upon those early disciples on the day of Pentecost.

First, the filling of the Spirit turned those early disciples into evangelists. As a result of the witness of those early disciples, about 3,000 souls were added to the church on that day and those who were added were those *"who gladly received **His word**."* (Acts 2: 41)

Second, the Holy Spirit produced a hunger and a thirst to know more about Christ and the Christian life. The Scripture tells us clearly that those who were saved on the day of Pentecost *"continued **steadfastly** in the apostles' **doctrine** and **fellowship**, in the **breaking of bread**, and in **prayers**."* (Acts 2: 42) The believer who would grow in the grace and knowledge of our Lord must never tire of learning about His doctrine. That is so absolutely basic to growing as a Christian! Those early Christians were literally **hungering and thirsting** after righteousness (Matthew 5: 6). So, we learn here that the power of the Holy Spirit and Biblical doctrine go hand in hand.

Third, there was a new level of fellowship. There had been periods of broken fellowship even among the disciples. Many times the disciples had displayed a selfish concern for greatness. Once they came to Jesus asking, *"Who will be the **greatest** in the kingdom of heaven?"* (Matthew18: 1) When Jesus was making His final journey up to Jerusalem where He would be crucified, the Mother of James and John approached Him and asked, *"that these two sons of mine may sit, one on Your right hand and the other on the left in your kingdom."* (Matthew 20:21) When the other disciples heard it they were *"moved with indignation against the two brothers."* (Verse 24) After these disciples had engaged in prayer and supplication for 10 days, the Holy Spirit fell upon them. They learned that a key factor in the fellowship of believers is that believers must **die to self.** There can be no real fellowship among believers if they are all self-centered and narcissitic. There can be no dying to self apart from the **infilling of the Holy Spirit.** That was a thing that plagued the church at Corinth and that is the reason that Paul pleaded with them to *"speak the same thing"* and that *"there be no divisions among you."* He wanted them to be *"perfectly joined together in the same mind."* (I Corinthians 1: 9-13) If the Holy Spirit is grieved, there will always be a **contrary spirit.**

Fourth, the fullness of the Spirit enabled the apostles to do *"many wonders and signs."* (Acts 2: 43) Those disciples who had, at one time, retreated behind closed doors were now a **flame of fire for Christ.** When they were **filled with the Holy Spirit** they *"turned the world upside down"* for Christ. (Acts 17: 6)

Fifth, the Holy Spirit gave those early Christians a holy boldness that they had never known before. Even in the midst of **persecution** they continued to go to the temple **daily** and to break bread from house to house. They didn't allow persecution to stop them. They *"did eat their meat with gladness and singleness of heart."* (Acts 2: 46) They were also *"praising God and having favor with all the people and the Lord added to the church **daily** those who were being saved."* (Verse 47)

When Peter and John were called on the carpet for the healing of the lame man and their preaching in the temple on Solomon's Porch, it was Peter, the man who at one time warmed himself by the enemies' fire in Caiaphas' palace and denied the Lord three times in his moment of cowardice, made answer to them saying, *"Let it be known to you all and to all the people of Israel, that by the name of Jesus Christ of Nazareth, whom you crucified, whom **God** raised from the dead, by **Him** this man stands before you **whole."*** (Acts 4: 10) What he said was certainly not popular among those who were gathered there but Peter now has a new **courage** and the **Holy Spirit** made the **difference!**

When they saw the **boldness** of Peter and John, and *"seeing the man who had been healed standing with them, they could say nothing against it."* (Verse 14) When their accusers took counsel among themselves, their conclusion was that a great miracle had occurred and they said, *"We cannot deny it."* That is the kind of thing that happens when Christians seek and are filled with the **power** of the **Holy Spirit**.

Threatening Priests

When the Priests threatened them and demanded that they not speak in the **name of Jesus** anymore, **Peter and John's** answer was, *"We cannot but speak the things which we have seen and heard."* (Acts 4: 20) If we would learn from John, that is the kind of man he was and he would not be silent about Jesus in order to please **anyone**. He was a loving man but he was firm and unbending in his conviction that Jesus was the Christ. How did they respond to the demands of the Priest? They went to God in prayer asking, *"Grant to your servants that with all boldness they may speak Your word."* (Verse 29) In verse 30 they asked for power to perform great things in *"the name of your holy servant Jesus."* What kind of answer did they receive? The answer was that *"The place where they were assembled together was shaken; and they were all filled with the Holy Spirit and they spoke the word of God with boldness."* (Verse 31) This is another example of an **infilling** of the **Holy Spirit**.

After the incident with Ananias and Sapphira, the apostles were gathered on Solomon's Porch where the people magnified them and believers were *"increasingly added to the Lord, multitudes both of men and women."* (Acts 5: 14) So powerful was the Holy Spirit in their lives that the people began bringing the sick and laying them in the path so that they might be healed when the **shadow** of Simon Peter passed over them. When the temple guards came and seized them and placed them in a common prison, an **angel** delivered them during the night. The next morning, when the guards found them **not** in the prison but **preaching** in the **name of Jesus** out in the temple area, the High Priest, the Chief Priest and the Captain of the temple became almost apoplectic. The Captain and the other officers went out to bring them to the council but they took them quietly because they feared that they would be stoned by the people. Then the High Priest said something that was very revealing when he said, *"Did not we strictly command you not to teach in this **name**? And look, you have **filled** Jerusalem with your **doctrine** and intend to bring this man's blood on us!"* (Acts 5: 28) It was then that Peter and the other apostles answered boldly saying, *"We ought to **obey God** rather than **men**. The God of our fathers raised up **Jesus** whom you **murdered** by hanging on a tree. **Him God has exalted** to His right hand to be prince and savior, to give repentance to Israel and forgiveness of sin. We are **witnesses** to these things, and so also is the **Holy Spirit** whom God has given to those who **obey Him**."* (Verse 32) The council disposed of the matter by beating the apostles and threatening them again. The response of the apostles to the beating was a **jewel for all ages**. They *"departed from the presence of the council, **rejoicing** that they were counted **worthy** to suffer **shame for His name**."* What a difference the Spirit made! (Acts 5: 41) The question for every believer in this age must be, "Are we ready to suffer **shame** for **His name in times like these**?"

Conclusion

Those early Christians had a hunger and thirst for the power of the Holy Spirit in their lives. They knew that the **boldness** that it takes to speak out, when no one else will, can only come through the power of the **Holy Spirit**. They continued for 10 days in

prayer and supplication until finally the Spirit came upon them on the day of Pentecost. That thirst that Jesus promised would be satisfied when the gift of the Holy Spirit was realized by them (John 7: 38). Let us never forget, as we have stated earlier in this chapter, that the Holy Spirit is ours for the asking. When a believer of today receives the Holy Spirit in his life he will have the same kind of boldness that those early apostles experienced. Simon Peter, who once cowered in fear and denied the Lord three times became one of the boldest proclaimers of the Gospel the world has ever known. The Holy Spirit may not be something that you can see with the naked eye but the results of His presence and work are obvious when he fills your life. A.J. Sims, in his hymn, "The Unseen Hand", says it well:

> "There is an unseen hand to me,
> That leads through ways I cannot see;
> While going through this world of woe,
> This hand still leads me as I go.
> I'm trusting to the unseen hand,
> That guides me through this weary land;
> And some sweet day I'll reach that strand
> Still guided by the unseen hand."

About The Author

Robert Tenery

He graduated from Pfeiffer University with a BA Degree and from Southwestern Baptist Theological Seminary with a MDiv. He pastored Baptist Churches for 40 years and is now retired. At the end of his active ministry he served seven and a half years as a Chaplain for the State of North Carolina in which he dealt with the most serious Juvenile Offenders in the State including those who had committed First Degree Murder, First Degree Rape, Armed Robbery, Car Jackings, Arson, Grand Larceny and other crimes. During the last six months he served he saw 61 of those young men become Christians and several are now in the ministry.

He also edited **The Southern Baptist** Advocate which went to 64,000 Southern Baptist Pastors and Lay Leaders during the Conservative Resurgence in the Southern Baptist Convention. He has done Ghost Writing for several individuals and has penned some poetry. He served as a Trustee of the Baptist Sunday School Board (Lifeway Christian Resources) for 16 years during which time the Trustees turned the Board back to its' historical roots, brought major improvements to the Sunday School Literature, purchased the Holman Bible Company and revamped the Bookstore System. It was also during his tenure there that the name of the Board was changed to Lifeway Christian Resources although he was never convinced that a change in jargon would solve all the problems.

He was privileged to attend meetings of the North American Mission Board where his wife served as a Trustee for eight years and enjoyed the exchange of ideas with other Pastors and Lay Leaders from across the Country. He also served as Vice-President of the Southern Baptist Pastors Conference and President of the North Carolina Baptist Pastors Conference. He served on the Committee on Boards for the SBC, the Church Growth Commission for the North Carolina Convention and the Governor's Commission on Infant Mortality as well as the Juvenile Crime Commission. During his last pastorate, he served on the County's Social Services Board and was Chairman when his tenure ended

Made in the USA
Middletown, DE
23 October 2016